D0498540

# GIVING

# GIVING

### PURPOSE
*is the*
### NEW
### CURRENCY

———

A L E X A N D R E   M A R S

**HarperOne**
*An Imprint of* HarperCollins*Publishers*

HarperOne

**100% of the author's proceeds will go the Epic portfolio organizations to help disadvantaged youth.**

HarperCollins books may be purchased for educational, business, or sales promotional use. For information, please email the Special Markets Department at SPsales@harpercollins.com.

Originally published as *La revolution du partage* in France in 2018 by FLAMMARION.

FIRST EDITION

*Designed by Yvonne Chan*

---

Library of Congress Cataloging-in-Publication Data

Names: Mars, Alexandre, author.
Title: Giving : purpose is the new currency / Alexandre Mars.
Other titles: Revolution du partage. English
Description: First edition. | New York, NY : HarperOne, [2018] | "Originally
   published as La revolution du partage in France in 2018 by Flammarion."
Identifiers: LCCN 2018045878 | ISBN 9780062912404 (hardcover)
Subjects: LCSH: Charities—History. | Social action.
Classification: LCC HV25 .M3613 2018 | DDC 361.7—dc23 LC record available at
   https://lccn.loc.gov/2018045878

---

19 20 21 22 23   LSC   10 9 8 7 6 5 4 3 2 1

# Contents

Contents

The opposite of poverty is not wealth.
The opposite of poverty is sharing.

—ABBE PIERRE

# Introduction

For the past few years, I've been traveling the world, asking any-one and everyone two questions. The scene often plays out like this:

I'll say, "Raise your hand if over the past year, you have given to charity." The hands go up.

I continue, "Now keep your hand in the air if you think you have given enough."

An awkward silence fills the air. Almost everyone lowers their hand. People look right and left, perhaps to reassure them-selves that all their neighbors have also lowered their arms. Per-haps because they somehow feel something is off. This happened everywhere I went. From recent graduates in Bogotá to execs in London, everyone felt they had more to give.

Before these two questions took over my life, I had worked tirelessly for twenty-five years to launch and develop start-ups. I wasn't always successful—I've been laughed out of more than one boardroom and have struggled to pay my bills. But sometimes I got lucky, and experience eventually taught me the valuable lesson of how to detect trends before they became mainstream. When early web browsers got more user-friendly, I bet my life savings on creating a web design agency. When 3G phones were launching in South Korea, I figured brands would start marketing on mobile phones and formed a mobile ad agency. Later, roughly around the time Myspace was overtaken by Facebook, I turned my eyes to commercial social media management. Yet despite my financial success, I rarely left work feeling fulfilled. My parents—especially my mother—always taught the importance of looking out for others and giving back. In my adult life, my wife—whose volunteer work has always inspired me—and I made sure to pass on these values to our children. But my goal was very clear when I started working: I had to make money quickly to get my freedom and then be able to devote the rest of my life to helping others. I soon realized this first objective then I was able to start a new chapter in my life.

In 2013, I decided to change everything and embark on a journey to learn about the world's issues from the people working on the ground. Eventually, I found that our best strategy was to learn how to share.

It took me awhile to find the reason for the disconnect between how much we *want* to give and how much we *actually* give. I am an entrepreneur, and if five start-ups and twenty-five years have taught me one lesson, it is to look at a situation in terms of where people are—our point A—and where people want to be—our point B. When I traveled around the world meeting shareholders, specialists, foundations, officials, social entrepreneurs and donors, I asked them what they needed, what obstacles they faced. I did this because I wanted to figure out their current and pressing reality: what was their point A, and what was keeping them from their point B? I learned that non-governmental organizations (NGOs) didn't just need funding, but unrestricted grants as well. I learned that most people want to donate, but between family and work they never find time to research charities. Observing the obstacles that prevented donors from giving more, I narrowed the problem down to three causes: lack of trust, lack of time, and lack of knowledge.

In a world where management scandals and corruption regularly undermine our trust, people are skeptical of financial governance. During my research travels, people often brought up scandals, from United Way's CEO siphoning donations to pay for his girlfriend's vacations back in the early '90s to the American Breast Cancer Foundation's president paying her son's telemarketing company millions to generate donations. Nonprofits are held to higher standards because of their mission-driven goals. Any one scandal sets everyone back. Additionally, the difficulty of demonstrating their impact and increasing their reach combined with their lack of transparency and accountability makes it difficult for nonprofits to restore donor confidence. As a result, people don't trust the known social organizations they *could* fund, and they lack the time and resources necessary to determine which ones deserve their support.

There is an added problem when considering the elite connotations of philanthropy: in a culture where people are constantly asked to donate to churches, schools, hospitals, and disaster relief, "giving more" is not an easy motto to promote. On top of that, the US is experiencing a time of increased economic inequality. According to the Pew Research Center, wealth gaps between upper-income families and lower- and middle-income families are at the highest levels ever recorded. The rising wealth gap means that disposable income in the middle class is shrinking. The very word "philanthropy" becomes attached to a privileged few with millions to spare. But philanthropy shouldn't be aspirational: it should be accessible and personal. Enabling people to give more is not just about increasing the amount of donations—it is about changing the way we look at giving and the way we practice it.

Not everything I learned was flavored by doom and gloom—I was shocked by the number of young people passionately and selflessly giving their time and money for the causes they cared about. I saw kids making signs and marching for women's rights and teenagers asking their friends to donate to charities instead of sending birthday presents. There is a growing desire to share, a positive drive to reach out. In fact, we are experiencing an era of unprecedented giving, with total American charitable giving exceeding $400 billion for the first time in recorded history in 2017. But this isn't the time to pat ourselves on the back for a job well done—there is still room for growth. Now is the time to take giving a step further.

After three years of research, I founded a nonprofit organization called Epic to address these problems. Revolutionizing the way we give comes down to two pivotal changes: giving better, and giving more.

*Better* is a relative term: I use it to imply that the way we give today is *inefficient.* Too few nonprofits clearly state what they aim to achieve, fewer still sufficiently measure their progress, and even fewer accurately and convincingly demonstrate their impact. Epic's job is to find the nonprofits that do all these things.

In the interest of selectivity, we built a powerful due-diligence system similar to the venture capital process of shortlisting prospective investments. We visited hundreds of organizations to see the reality of their struggles on the ground and to encounter unsung heroes.

"Giving better" also means giving that does not stop when you mail a check or click SEND. We needed to change the way donors experience their impact. This led us to explore how to measure impact, how to report on it, and how to relay that information back to the donor. From virtual reality to news apps, field trips, and multidimensional reporting, we have worked to bridge the gap between donors and beneficiaries.

The search for new avenues of philanthropy brought us to explore workplace giving through painless payroll deductions—like a 401(k) for donating to nonprofits that employers can match. It brought me to examine the possibilities at cashiers and checkout counters where a few cents every now and then—always optional, but always an option—could create a tangible social impact when placed in the right hands. We need to make it possible for every sector—from finance to retail—to embrace giving through approaches that fit the way they make money. By bringing together pledges and initiatives tailored for them, we can convince them to join us in this new giving journey.

And it works. Or more accurately, it is beginning to work. In companies that promote payroll giving, employees sign up in great numbers. At Dior, about a quarter of employees now give every month, and the company aims to reach 50 percent by the end of the year. While rolling out these solutions at L'Oréal and Coca-Cola, we've seen the same mind-set developing: simple, painless solutions with a tangible impact on the lives of others will make people more inclined to give.

Entrepreneurs are also rallying to sign pledges: from veterans of Silicon Valley like Evernote's Phil Libin to newcomers like Boxed's Chieh Huang, businessmen who should just be preoccupied with their bottom line are making sure their practices are socially responsible.

With Epic, I want to reinvent sharing as something accessible, efficient, and impactful. But this is not just the story of Epic, it's the story of a growing movement fueled by a younger generation driven to enact social change. We need to change the way we think about philanthropy in order to create systemic change. Sharing needs to become transformational and natural: a way of life that will bring us back together. This is about everyday people choosing to change the way they think about giving, not billionaires donating millions. By asking those in power to make giving a part of their platform, and by making a tiny lifestyle change to be more generous, we can amplify the impact of countless nonprofits doing effective work.

With technology, we can change the experience of giving and achieve these goals. I grew up in a world where what connected donors to charities were dimes that went into a donation box on the counter and annual mailings brought by USPS from institutional charities with a few facts and a request for a check. A world where, if you were lucky, you could use Dad's PC in the basement and a mailed-in AOL CD to dial up and browse a few pages on Netscape until your Mom had to use the phone. Today, I can video chat with my family in Brooklyn while visiting an NGO in Kampala on a phone not much heavier than a bag of Skittles.

Technology is slowly making its way into the philanthropic sector. Facebook and Google have both started allowing users to request donations for causes they care about from friends. Websites like GoFundMe allow people and organizations to reach interested donors directly. These organizations prove that technology can make philanthropy more accessible and effective. Now we need to expand the reach of these tools. That is the only way to achieve systemic change. If we all work, each in their own way, to their own extent, to open ourselves up to others and share our time, money, and skills, we can build a more just and encouraging world.

The momentum is growing. It is emerging in a world where purpose is the new currency, where we measure the value of our deeds by their social impact. That world is our new hope. Together, let's embrace it.

# 1

# Purpose Redefined

> "As we look ahead into the next century,
> leaders will be those who empower others."
>
> —BILL GATES

Facing me is a young man, the son of Dominican immigrants. He served in the US Army, then attended Columbia University. I'm interviewing him for a position at my holding tech group. I ask him why he wants to work in finance.

"I want my success to help other people," he answers.

Ten years ago, the same person would have replied, with equal sincerity, "I want to earn a lot of money."

I still can't quite believe it. I'm used to answering questions like: Will I have my own office? How's the view? What's the company car? *Me, myself,* and *I*—those were the main considerations. Generations Y—the millennials—and Z would rather talk about meaning, about purpose, about sharing. They want to know what the company will do with its profits. Pour them all into share dividends? That's not good enough for them.

A recent survey showed that 20 percent of Stanford undergraduates want to work for a social enterprise—for companies that care and maintain transparency about their social impact. Ten years ago, I'm guessing that the percentage of students who wanted to work in that sector was pretty close to zero. Now, even the other 80 percent would prefer to work for socially responsible companies.

Fifty percent of the world's current population is under thirty years old. Very soon, Generations Y and Z will represent half of the global workforce—and they will change the rules of the game.

Contrary to popular belief, the young people who make up these generations work hard. I see it in my own employees day in and day out. They are willing to put in the effort, but they have no illusions: they need money to live, to pay their rent, but they are not going to give twenty or thirty years of their lives to the company, nor will they sacrifice their personal existence for a job as their predecessors did. They will sign a deal for two or three years. After that, who knows?

Younger generations are coming of age in a world marked by insecurity. They've inherited a rapidly changing economy and a planet struggling with climate change. Yet despite the unknowns, they have united in the face of adversity and fought for the world they deserve. After the shootings at the Bataclan in Paris, they gathered, spontaneously, in the Place de la République to light candles. After Parkland, they held hands and marched on Washington. Together, they felt strong. They believe in sharing, in solidarity.

The first signs of their social disruption occurred when they became numerous enough to factor in the labor market. A few years from now, they will be in charge. Generations Y and Z do not have the luxury of being self-seeking. They are not stupid—they can see that political and economic power no longer reside solely in religions and governments; these days, power is also in the hands of companies, some of which are more powerful than many states. Young people today can see that multinational companies have an unprecedented ability to act. Consequently, they expect these companies to take their responsibilities seriously—because they have not only the means, but above all the duty, to do so. These young people are ready to form armies of volunteers. To earn slightly less, if that's what it takes to do meaningful work. And, if they do earn a lot of money, to give some purpose to those zeros on their paycheck.

This is a radical paradigm shift. For the first time, companies are not just responding to shifts in the market. Millennials' more socially responsible worldview and purpose-driven perspective have increasingly forced company recruiters to become aware of their new, expanded role within society and to adapt to it. Their efforts have been ungraceful and at times painful, but they are forcing real change.

My fellow members of Generation X have also discovered insecurity. They have to some extent started looking farther than their own navels and their own futures, and they have begun to enter the age of questioning: what have they done with their lives? They, too, have lost the desire to work in a business that has no meaning. I have seen this play out in my own experience:

Myriam Vander Elst, the stellar head of Epic's European operations, used to head up strategy for several global brands. "I earn less than before," she explained to me, "but my life has so much more purpose now. I finally feel at home."

Giving is no longer just the prerogative or duty of older people: charity must become inclusive, something that unites rather than divides the generations.

I have seen this on countless occasions. One Friday, I gave a presentation at the offices of Coca-Cola. I watched as employees entered and filled the room, occupying all the chairs, all the stools, and then the floor. Many of them were young, but there were also plenty of older executives. People with gray hair: baby-boomers, close to retirement, encouraged to attend by people the same age as their children. Some even admitted to me that they did not really understand what was happening: they had never imagined that one day, the urge to give would become so strong—least of all that they would feel this urge themselves.

In 2017, I started meeting with venture-capital funds to suggest they join the Epic Sharing Pledge, giving a small percentage of their capital gains—even as little as 1 percent—to social causes. I met the managers of ten funds, seven of whom enthusiastically agreed to my proposal. That success encouraged me to raise the bar by extending our Sharing Pledge to private equity investment funds. As usual, I knocked on doors.

In London, when Pierre-Antoine de Selancy asked his two cofounders of the 17Capital investment fund whether they wished to join, their response was immediate: yes. They were ready to give 1 percent of the carried interest on one of their funds, which alone amounted to $1.4 billion.

They in turn put the same question to the twenty-five employees (average age: thirty) who were beneficiaries of this carried interest. "We gave everyone a free choice," Pierre-Antoine explained to me. "We expected several people to commit to the pledge, but we could never have imagined that twenty-three of the twenty-five would say yes to giving away part of their profits, not just voluntarily but enthusiastically."

The clients of 17Capital primarily include institutions, such as pension funds and insurance companies. They might easily have remained indifferent to this proposal, which added nothing to their profits, but in fact they reacted quickly and positively. "Very few investors these days consider ethics and values to be optional," Pierre-Antoine told me. "Selfishness no longer raises funds. Everyone is aware that government treasuries are empty and that it is up to us—civil society, entrepreneurs, investors—to take over from the welfare state. Giving has to become the norm. The situation is urgent."

Pierre-Antoine de Selancy plans to extend the Epic Sharing Pledge to other funds managed by 17Capital, and he is enthusiastic about the prospect. After all, sharing runs in his blood: his mother received the Legion of Honour for her forty-year commitment to the Red Cross. "I am happy to carry the torch," he adds with a smile.

This need for purpose exists among the teams at both of my businesses. In fact, even after Sam Giber, a young prodigy and Epic's first employee, transferred to blisce/ to hone the investment skills he had learned at school and as a young entrepreneur, he retained the sense of purpose in his job. Romain Sion, another trailblazing member of blisce/, spends three weeks every summer on the ground to study the impact of our Epic portfolio organizations. He went to India in 2016 to visit Apnalaya, to the countryside of Uganda the next year to visit orphans of Nyaka, and recently to Nairobi, Kenya to assist the social workers of Carolina for Kibera, another organization in our portfolio. The teams at blisce/ and Epic aim to nurture a vibrant culture of social impact in the investment community. When in the same city, the two teams work side by side, and they share the same mind-set: they are driven by purpose, not the desire to make more money.

# 2

# The Evolving History of Giving

> "My religion is very simple.
> My religion is kindness."
>
> —DALAI LAMA

For millennia, giving back has been the domain of various religions—and, undoubtedly, a way for religious leaders to avoid social disorder during periods when religious and political power operated together. They theorized about giving, made it part of their doctrines, and transformed it into an essential step on the path to salvation.

This goes back long before the advent of monotheism.

In the Egypt of the Pharaohs, the principle of *maat*—the principle of truth and justice, described by the Egyptologist Jan Assmann as "the invention of virtue"—involved living an honest life and helping those worse off. People considered *maat*, which includes the obligation to share, a necessary condition for achieving immortality (along with the financial means to commission a tomb).

During the same period, in Babylon, part of each house of divinity—the temples where the gods were worshipped—devoted itself to looking after the poor, the sick, widows, and orphans, giving them food and lodging, even setting aside a portion of donations collected for the divine cult.

In Southern Asia, Buddha famously told his disciple Rahula: "If you knew what I know about the power of giving, you would not let a single meal pass without sharing it in some way." In the Indo-Aryan Pali language, *dana*—generosity—constitutes the first of the ten perfections and the first of the three great meritorious actions (the other two being moral behavior and meditation). *Dana* should be directed, in order of importance, toward friends and family, then the poor and the helpless (among them animals), and lastly monks. Training ourselves to give, say the Buddhists, enables us to detach ourselves from the material goods that connect us to the cycle of rebirth, and to also better understand the world around us in order to develop a benevolent love for it and to weaken anger, hatred, and pride. Buddhists still consider *dana* the height of wisdom, the expression of the individual's evolution on the path to perfection.

In Judaism, the *tzedakah*—literally, the act of justice, with the intention of repairing natural and social inequities—is obligatory. It is a divine commandment. Even the poor man who receives alms must share them with those poorer than him. The rabbis fixed the rate at a minimum of 10 percent of income; and the Zohar, the foundational work in the literature of Jewish mystical thought known as Kabbalah, states that when a poor person begs for alms, we must thank God for offering us the opportunity to be generous. He who gives—the Tzadik, or the Just—is considered to stand at the summit of the human pyramid.

During the first centuries of Christianity, the Church organized charity through monasteries where bishops would draw up registers of the poor, who would receive food, clothes, and lodging. Charity was considered a divine commandment and no devout Christian would imagine foregoing it. In the Middle Ages, a mandatory deduction of the tithe—10 percent of income—became law. Today, the word *tithe* has disappeared from the vocabulary of the devout Christian (and with it the 10 percent obligation) in favor of the word *offering* (a voluntary donation).

Islam, too, conforms to the rule of charity with the *zakat*, one of the five pillars of Islam, mentioned in more than eighty verses of the Quran. The *zakat* corresponds to 2.5 percent of the income of each believer: not only an act of generosity, it represents purification of the believer's belongings and of his soul, distancing him from the sins of avarice and greed. In most cases, the *zakat* goes to poor people living in the same region as the donor.

From the nineteenth century onward, the modern nation-state began to take over from religious institutions as the primary arbiter of wealth redistribution. Income tax replaced the tithe, and the faithful became less generous toward the church. In some countries, notably in Europe and Latin America, the government still imposes a "religious tax" as well as a civil tax. In Germany, the Kirchensteuer represents between 8 and 9 percent of income tax—in other words, between 0.2 and 1.5 percent of total income. Austria, Argentina, and Denmark apply the rate of 1 percent of income. This can rise to as much as 2.3 percent in Switzerland or Finland, but is much lower in Italy (0.85 percent). In secular countries like France that do not impose a religious tax, churches have been reporting a steady decline in donations for decades.

I've been asked whether Epic and the growing charity system are attempting to replace religion, both in terms of the quest for meaning and the collection of donations. This question surprises me. Our objective is not to replace anything: we offer a complementary service, to religions as well as governments. There is no "or" when it comes to generosity: the responsibility belongs not to one group of people or another but to all of us. Governments redistribute wealth to some degree, and religions organize a form of charity with their means. But they no longer possess most of the world's wealth. These days, the world's riches are in the hands of private companies. We need to redirect our attentions to holding them accountable.

A good example of this is India, the first country to write companies' social responsibilities into the law. Since 2014, any business with annual revenues of more than $160 million, or with yearly profits over $830,000, must pay 2 percent of that profit to programs of their choice, whether NGOs or charity organizations. According to figures provided by the *Economic Times*, corporations have redirected $2 billion annually to social programs—without anyone asking whether these programs will one day replace Hindu temples or the Indian government.

This is an incredible and successful instance of using the powers of government to ensure corporate social responsibility. This legislation is replicable beyond India and should be encouraged.

We must change our mind-set towards giving. Gifts do not have to replace one another; they can add to and complete one another.

# 3

# Citizens, Consumers, Workers

"When a country is well governed, poverty and a
mean condition are something to be ashamed of.
When a country is ill governed, riches and
honors are something to be ashamed of."

—CONFUCIUS

I believe in government. I do not believe in a world where governments no longer exist or where they are stripped to bare bones, as some libertarians demand.

We need government: it provides us with security, peace, rules, laws, and structures; it manages the public spaces that belong to all of us. In a number of countries, the government offers free schooling, free universities, free healthcare, opportunity for all, and a certain vision of equality. In other countries, it plays an admittedly more modest role, but it remains indispensable for all the same reasons.

But money and power no longer belong exclusively to national governments; they now also reside in the hands of businesses. Corporations are not governments and should not replace them, but we do need to adjust the way we think about global power. For the ship of this world to navigate the choppy waters ahead, we must quickly put another system in place—a hybrid model that has not yet been invented—that will hold corporations accountable to their communities and encourage, if not obligate, them to contribute. All of us now have power not just as citizens but as consumers and workers. We need to leverage each of these roles in order to fight systemic injustice.

When thinking about philanthropy, we need to address the new global economic and political reality. We need to work with both businesses and governments. We must take the best from the private sector—funding and the connections between employees and clients—while working hand in hand with the public sector and making the most of the precious support offered by local authorities, local employment offices, and so on.

I have seen this at play with Epic. We support SNEHA, an NGO working in India to prevent suicide, the third most common cause of death in the country, particularly among women. When we help SNEHA to fund action groups that empower women to fight against domestic violence and sexual assault, we need local governments to protect the volunteers and social workers and to pass and enforce laws. We cannot operate without their support.

In Cambodia and Thailand, we work alongside Friends-International, whose mission is to rescue street children from the grips of prostitution, drugs, and poverty; to give them food and a roof and, above all, access to education and the chance of legitimate employment. All of this requires funding from the private sector, but we also benefit from the aid given by government organizations and structures: the judiciary, the police, and the countries' hospitals, schools, and training centers.

I regularly hear people of all income levels call themselves philanthropists. When I ask them which charities they support, they reply: "I pay my taxes." This way of thinking exasperates me. I pay my taxes too, of course, but this is not an act of philanthropy—it is an act of citizenship. Merely paying my taxes is not enough. I cannot and will not accept a world where your place of birth may condemn you to a life of poverty, a life without opportunity. Because I pay taxes, my children can go to school and I can drive on paved roads, but giving should have more to do with our desire for justice than our personal needs and preferences. We need governments; we need taxes. But we also need to do more outside of our basic roles as citizens.

# 4

# A Global Change

"We make a living by what we get.
We make a life by what we give."
—WINSTON S. CHURCHILL

In the 1980s, 1990s, and 2000s, when we calculated success only by the number of companies in a stock market portfolio, greed dominated the world of business. I met so many people driven purely by the desire to increase the zeros in their bank account—people I jokingly called "Scrooges" under my breath. People accumulating for the sake of accumulating, always greedy for more, never wanting to share. People with no regard for empathy or the common good, who knew the old rules of business and economics and showed little interest in anything that did not directly affect them.

Only a decade ago, such greed-driven workers seemed unstoppable. Now I look around and see them as an endangered species. Certainly it is not only a question of age: some young entrepreneurs similarly believe that the world belongs to them. But increasingly we see a younger generation driven more by purpose than by money. The fact is, people know today what they didn't know yesterday: That half of the world's wealth belongs to 1 percent of its inhabitants. That four-fifths of the world's people survive on less than 5 percent of its resources. That a shamefully small percentage of property is shared. Young people can see injustices clearly, and they cannot ignore them.

I witnessed the beginnings of this change in mind-set in the late 1990s. For years, Nike had been lambasted for conditions inside its subcontracted factories, particularly in Pakistan. In 1997, just as the brand's annual revenue exceeded $1 billion for the first time, a photograph was seen all over the world: a child squatting on the floor of a poverty-stricken factory, sewing together soccer balls stamped with the famous Nike swoosh. Protests and boycotts erupted around the world and Nike had no choice: to keep selling its products and prevent its revenues from falling through the floor, the company was forced to introduce more ethical practices and to impose work standards on all its subcontractors. In 1998, then-CEO Phil Knight pledged to allow labor and human rights groups to investigate the company's contractors and factories. Its competitors Reebok and adidas, whose business practices were no better than Nike's, had to fall in line too. In 2017, protests again erupted around the world after Nike laid off unionized workers in Honduras and reports of wage theft occurred in Vietnam. These protests were led mainly by American university students who managed to convince their schools to end sports apparel contracts

with Nike. Nike once again agreed to allow in third-party in-
vestigators and pressured local factory owners. These changes
were expensive, and they only came under pressure. But companies are now quickly realizing that if they don't become more
ethical and responsible, consumers will leave and spend their
dollars elsewhere.

# 5

# The New Business Leaders

"No one has ever become poor by giving."

—ANNE FRANK

There have always been business leaders who cared about more than their bottom line. In the nineteenth and early twentieth centuries, these paternalistic bosses were common. Anticipating changes in the law, they ensured the well-being of their workers: lodging them in decent conditions, providing medical care, educating and then employing their children, and even showing a concern for their leisure activities. They often drew motivation from their Christianity, the sense of carrying out a mission. In Britain, George Cadbury created the garden city of Bournville close to Birmingham; in France, you had the Michelins in Clermont-Ferrand; in Germany, the Krupps; in the United States, Henry Ford.

Although they almost vanished between the two world wars, when many governments made social protection a prerogative, these activist-bosses have begun coming back out of the woodwork, and that sense of mission still drives them. In our globalized world, they no longer operate on a local level, but see the entire planet as a village. The most famous example is that of Bill Gates, who in 1997 created a foundation to provide internet access for libraries and, after coming upon a newspaper article about the millions of children who were dying due to a lack of basic healthcare, signed a check for $100 million to finance a mass vaccination program. In 2000, he formalized his commitment to the idea of sharing by creating the Bill & Melinda Gates Foundation. Traveling all over the world, he intensified his battle against poverty. Since 2008, he and his wife, Melinda, have devoted themselves full-time to this cause—and they are not the only ones. Not everyone can write a check for $100 million, of course, but there are other bosses who give what they can.

We also see business leaders who distribute their wealth simply because it is in their interest to do so. Perhaps they face pressure from their family and friends, and their children in particular. Or from their employees, who demand accountability. Or from their customers: it has never been easier for every one of us to change our supplier for any given product. Uber suffered these consequences, losing a considerable part of its market share when other options like Lyft emerged that functioned just as well but were more generous with their drivers and required no more effort from their new clients than the thirty seconds it took to download the app on their phone.

Ultimately, the results matter more than the motivations. Selfishness? We're all selfish to some degree. A business plan? It's natural for businesspeople to do whatever they can to ensure the prosperity of their companies in the face of increased competition. Religion, culture, education? All important influences, but the essential thing, for me, is that people have realized their economic ventures can no longer disregard social action.

The entrepreneur Rakesh Tondon sets a perfect example of the new kind of philanthropist we need. He already donated regularly to a number of charities, but he wished to combine his generosity with a certain rationality.

Rakesh was born and raised in India, the son of a well-off family. His father was a dentist and his mother was a social worker. Rakesh had great respect for his mother's work, where she essentially gave women and children a second chance at life. She made sure they had access to education and healthcare. But most of all she treated each person that came into her office with respect and ensured the dignity of choice. Such ideas had surrounded Rakesh as a child and he could not imagine a life without social commitments.

He had completed his higher education in the United States and had spent twelve years working in the banking sector. An idea for a start-up had grown in his mind while his wife was pregnant: "She kept telling me, even more often than usual—and despite the fact that her closet was completely full of clothes—that she had nothing to wear." Le Tote—the Netflix of fashion (with a subscription rental system)—was born in 2012.

When I proposed to Rakesh that he join the Epic Sharing Pledge by giving a small percentage of his shares to good causes, I suggested 1 percent to start. He immediately raised the bar to 5 percent, while making it clear that he would not stop giving to the other charities he already supported. He aims to give 10 to 15 percent of his profits to charity and plans to increase that number down the road.

The day he signed his first big donation check, Rakesh admitted, "At first, it was hard. Imagine—the price of a nice car, or even a house! Then I looked around. I still had plenty left, after all. Enough to ensure my family had a good life. Did I really need more money? No. But I also remember the lightness I felt—it was so gratifying. I thought about the impact my gift could have. It gave me a strange feeling of satisfaction, which I wanted to share." And that was the key: giving had become joyful.

First, he talked about it to his friends: delicately to those friends who hadn't moved toward philanthropy, so as not to embarrass them; enthusiastically to those who were philanthropists themselves. "I tell them about my donations to encourage them to imitate me. To give more. To feel even more of that strange, wonderful emotion that accompanies the act of sharing."

Bertrand and Mathilde Thomas moved to New York at more or less the same time that I did, back in 2010. I was developing my start-up and they were launching Caudalie, their cosmetics brand, in North America. While I was still just focusing on launching my start-up, they were already championing environmental causes. In 2012, Caudalie would become the first European company to join the 1% for the Planet foundation by donating 1 percent of its global revenues to ecological charities.

They gave because they couldn't imagine *not* giving. But in doing so, they discovered some awkward roadblocks. Bertrand told me about his numerous disappointments with the charity world: money distributed poorly—or not distributed at all—meetings for the sake of meetings, ponderous speeches instead of effective action in the field, and the lack of clarity and accountability of many of the organizations. Yet they continued because, as they kept telling me, "It's shameful not to give."

Caudalie was one of the first companies to join the Epic movement. Even so, we did not have an environmental NGO in our portfolio. "But with Epic," Bertrand told me, "I know that 100 percent of what I give is really given. And I can follow the impact of our donation, day after day: the school that gets built, the first children who attend, the first diplomas they receive."

In three years, Caudalie donated $1 million through Epic to social causes in France, Thailand, and Vietnam, all while continuing to plant trees all over the world: by early 2018 they had planted four million. And they won't stop giving. "The young people who join our teams all say that they were drawn to us not only by our products and our working conditions but by our ethical values. And the day is coming when consumers will boycott the more selfish brands, the companies that have not made giving an integral part of their business structure. With 1 percent of our revenues going to social causes, the deal is clear: for every fifty euros that you pay us, fifty centimes will go to save the world. And that's perfectly normal."

These are the brands of the future.

We can force corporations to be more socially responsible. We can help the many private sector leaders who are ready to adapt but do not know how to go about it. Whether young start-up founders or more traditional CEOs, they all know it's in their best interest to share. Often, they have not taken the first step only because they do not know whom they should share with or how to proceed.

I had these bosses in mind when I launched Epic. I drew upon my years of experience and insight in the business and tech worlds. I knew that these companies value efficiency. So, Epic's solutions are made to be simple and painless to implement. Businesses are ultimately a numbers- and results-driven game. Therefore, a core part of Epic's philosophy is offering transparent methods of measuring social impact. Epic collects donations and then directs 100 percent of them toward social enterprises and NGOs chosen according to highly rigorous criteria. Other organizations like the American Red Cross have similar programs, but they are primarily focused on one issue or have transaction fees. I knew these stipulations could be deal breakers, so I strove to resolve them. In any case, the tactics Epic uses are transferable. We each have the power as leaders, employees, and consumers to advocate for simpler, more transparent ways of giving. We have all been swept up by the same wave.

This can go even further. I fund all of Epic's structural costs—as well as its offices and employees—which comes to a few million dollars per year, through the earnings of blisce/. As a result, 100 percent of the donations we receive go directly to charities. This completely new economic model has been a welcome success and given meaning to my employees' work. Other organizations can take this leap too; Epic proves that it is possible.

# 6

# Trust, Start-Ups, and Grandmas

"Love all, trust a few, do wrong to none."

—WILLIAM SHAKESPEARE

Throughout my time at Epic, I have noticed a trend of distrust toward nonprofits. I have heard people denigrate these organizations' abilities and hastily label them as amateurs. And yet, in the start-up world, I have seen some men and women give millions to twenty-five-year-olds without any experience to back up their ideas.

I have built my existence on trusting both.

I trust in a civil society that behaves maturely once it has been given the right information and helped to restructure itself.

I trust in companies' capacity to evolve, and I trust social entrepreneurs. I know that they have solutions and strive for excellence. I do not calculate the achievements of Epic or any charity organization solely in terms of the sums raised or the number of charities supported, because the human element will always be immeasurable. The important thing is that exceptional social enterprises exist and have tried and tested structures, frameworks that can be replicated and transferred to other businesses. Every week I discover a new such organization, whose vitality, ingenuity, and success stun me.

I am not naïve. I know that trusting people brings an element of risk. But it is my ability to trust that has allowed me to make my way in life.

In the world of nonprofits I have seen the greatest stories of trust. In the early 2000s, several villages in the south of Uganda, devastated by AIDS, were left with a strangely imbalanced population: destitute grandmothers who had not been touched by the epidemic because they were no longer sexually active, and half-starved orphans whose parents, uncles, and aunts had all been killed by the disease in the absence of any possible treatment. There are 1.1 million AIDS orphans in Uganda. Logically, neither the grandmothers nor the orphans had much chance of survival, since neither possessed any means of subsistence: as in most of the world's countries, the elderly in Uganda must rely entirely on the aid of their children, and those children had all died.

In an informal way, the grandmothers helped one another: the strongest ones planted a few vegetables, the others prepared meals or looked after the children, who grew up, but without any sort of future. An NGO named Nyaka took an interest in this situation. Founded in 2001 by Twesigye Jackson Kaguri, a Ugandan living in the United States who suddenly found himself responsible for the children of his brother and then of his sister, both of whom died from AIDS, Nyaka runs orphanages. But rather than taking the children away from those villages, they decided to trust the grandmothers.

Nyaka supported the informal groups of grandmothers with financial aid but left them completely autonomous, free to decide how to allocate the money they received. Some grandmothers received microcredits to start a business, others took part in agricultural training. Nyaka helped each village set up a kitchen, organize classes for the younger children, and establish basket-weaving or jewel-making workshops for older ones. People with computing knowledge were chosen to run an online store.

Today there are ninety-eight such groups, bringing together 7,300 grandmothers. No one would have given these women a chance when the disaster hit, but they have proven themselves brilliant managers. Nyaka's grandmother project, a crazy gamble, has ensured the rebirth of ninety-eight villages. It's incredible what a little trust can do.

# 7

# Tech: Everyone Can Be a Donor

"Technology is nothing. What's important is that
you have a faith in people, that they're basically
good and smart, and if you give them tools,
they'll do wonderful things with them."
—STEVE JOBS

Many aspects of our technological age pose serious problems. I admit I'm not too thrilled at the thought of being driven to a restaurant by a robot car, served by a robot waiter, and given food cooked by a robot chef. I am also not too thrilled by the idea of having my job stolen by a robot, and I find it hard to justify to my children that they should still learn a foreign language when they can simply download an app that will translate speech straight into their earbuds.

Less visible than this technological disruption—but likely just as consequential—the coming social disruption may cause us to reevaluate almost everything we know. The projected figures are terrifying. By 2025, 50 percent of today's jobs will no longer exist. We will create other jobs, but not enough to fill the void. We can already see the beginnings of an ecological crisis in the smog-filled air of Beijing and New Delhi, where schools often have to close because of elevated pollution levels, and this phenomenon will inevitably spread to other cities in Europe and the Americas. Add to this an impending political crisis (the rise of populism and the establishment of autocratic regimes even in countries that we might imagine immune to such distortions of democracy) and you behold a frightening picture.

On the other hand, some figures suggest that things are getting better. It is a fact that fewer people are dying from acts of violence than in the past. In the eighth century, the Western world saw 100 murders for every 100,000 inhabitants. This figure has now fallen to an all-time low of only 0.85 murders per 100,000 inhabitants—a fact not reflected in the rising feeling of insecurity spurred on by the accelerating spread of information. We continue to eradicate diseases like malaria and polio. HIV is no longer fatal in countries whose inhabitants have access to advanced treatments. The illiteracy and poverty rates are falling on a global scale. Millions of people around the world have risen into the middle class. We live in an age of great uncertainty but also great progress. It's complicated and confusing, but time and time again, I've been blown away by people's abilities to take on obstacles and succeed. We have to use this momentum and push forward. This is activism and, together with the tools technology affords, it can lead to systemic change.

Practically, technology can help in two ways: by improving our performance and by opening up new opportunities. In this process we must also differentiate between visible but superficial improvements and actual systemic change.

Like any sector, nonprofits have struggled with mismanagement, and even some of the most well-regarded charities have weathered scandals. The Wounded Warrior Project was founded in 2003 to serve US veterans and has since raised over a billion dollars. In 2016 the *New York Times* reported that only 40 percent of its revenues went to programs helping veterans—the rest was spent on overhead costs. To make matters worse, reports also emerged of extravagant parties for staff and executives. There is no hard-and-fast rule about the optimal proportion of overhead in the nonprofit world. Fundraising costs money. Offices, computers, travels, staff compensation, and benefits all must be paid for, and depending on the overall trajectory of the charity, its size, and its structure, the definition of "a healthy amount" can vary; but when almost every other dollar raised does not reach the beneficiaries, that stands out. To see that money wasted on parties revolts donors and dissuades them not only from giving to the Wounded Warrior Project, but from giving in general. Ultimately, any failure of management, even one that doesn't amount to a crime, is a loss for the mission and a missed opportunity to help beneficiaries.

The shortcomings of nonprofit organizations also extend beyond scandals. The philanthropic industry as a whole suffers from transparency issues. Through Epic's selection process, we have evaluated hundreds of nonprofits from around the world, and many organizations cannot even clearly explain what they are trying to achieve. Of the 4,000 organizations we looked at in our selection process, 40 percent did not have specific impact metrics, and 26 percent of them were not even measurable. How can we expect an organization to demonstrate an impact it has not even formalized?

We will always have underperforming and mismanaged charities because charity management, like any management, is a human enterprise subject to failure and incompetence. There will always be scandalous and criminal behavior because non-profit professionals can also be crooks or criminals, but at the same time they are held to higher standards. The good news is that we now have so many options in governance, monitoring, policy, analysis, and reporting for alleviating those risks that we can help lessen the instances that do occur. Donors deserve better, and beneficiaries must be assured that guidance and support will never come at the expense of their integrity, dignity, or humanity.

In the United States, about two-thirds of the over $400 billion annual donations go to local churches, temples, synagogues, schools, and hospitals. This staggering figure shows the strong ties that Americans enjoy with their communities, but it also reflects charities' inability to highlight the significance of causes farther from home. In an era of ubiquitous technology, this limitation should no longer exist. If we can locate a moving Lyft car within twenty feet in Kauai, then we can just as easily locate a Meals-on-Wheels distribution cab in Detroit. If UPS can send you a notification on your phone the second their driver drops your package at the door, you can just as easily follow in real time the number of vaccines administered by a field hospital in Kampala.

If you can livestream your niece's wedding in Myrtle Beach, you should be able to Skype into a Python class for underprivileged students. That technology exists; applying it to the philanthropic sector would break the constraint of local philanthropy by empowering people to have an impact around the world. Some charities have already made strides in that direction.

Charity: water is a New York–based nonprofit organization led by CEO Scott Harrison. Its mission to bring clean water to all those without access to it, and it places its projects mostly outside of the United States. They have faced the very obstacle of distance between donor and beneficiary described above. Charity: water resolved that problem by ensuring that each donor receives the details of the well their donation helped to dig, including the geographic coordinates on an online map. This focus on pinpointing impact has likely been instrumental to charity: water's success, with over $250 million raised so far. People want to make sure their donations reach the people who need them most and will participate more readily if given that reassurance. Additionally, charity: water's model means that 100 percent of public donations go to their projects. Overhead costs are covered by private donors and grants. Nonprofit watchdog organizations like Charity Navigator and Guidestar have given charity: water some of their highest ratings due to this radical transparency.

Fundraising provides another challenge for nonprofits that we can address simply by leveraging existing technology. Wherever we pay for goods, we should have the ability to donate as well. The reliability of payment processors—from online credit card transactions to NFC devices like Apple Pay, Samsung Pay, or

Google Pay—has been well established, so we have no excuse not to take full advantage of them. The launch of Facebook Donate offers a perfect example: Facebook has made it possible for organizations to collect donations through a simple "Donate" button, while Facebook handles the payment processing. This recent development simply extends an existing business model to include philanthropy. Google took a similar route when it opened its G Suite platform to all registered nonprofits free of charge.

In some cases, the availability of new technology has led to the emergence of innovative fundraising platforms like Go-FundMe. Essentially, such platforms exist to bring those seeking money closer to those looking to give. Conceptually, even technically, they still remain within the current paradigm: they channel a database of campaigns on web pages and apps to an audience, whose members can then browse and select the projects they wish to support. In other words, these platforms are facilitators. And for many philanthropic projects, they are helpful. But they do not address the selectivity of impact: nothing on these platforms will inform or advise donors on the strategic effectiveness of their donations. As a result, they improve the current paradigm but fail to disrupt the philanthropic sector in any lasting way.

Other aspects of the current nonprofit world can complement these improvements. For instance, sites which aim to create more transparency in nonprofits by parsing their mandatory federal reports, like Charity Navigator, bring valuable information on the financial side of organizations. Even pragmatic websites like Double the Donation, which helps donors use corporate matching to increase the overall level of employee donations, bring to the table a useful service—one that improves the status quo—but does not effect a paradigm shift.

Those improvements, while comforting, will not resolve the problems our world faces. That is why we need a new paradigm. And it is achievable through a new generation of technological tools. Issues of trust need no longer stand in the way. Donations will soon be traceable on a wallet-to-wallet basis and immediately accessible with the same ease as paying the babysitter with a swipe. Whether through blockchain-based technology or other channels, donors will be able to trace their money and their impact in a secure, two-way communication flow.

Action data will be immediately available and immersive. We will have easy and clear access to cost reports itemized between delivery, tax, and commissions, allowing for more informed and immediate decisions in the selection of beneficiaries. This will apply pressure to organizations lacking in transparency. It will force an unpacking of overhead costs. Donors will spend charity dollars the same way people select stocks, bonds, and ETFs online today, with all pertinent information on hand and with an allocation of resources that will evolve as the donor's concerns and interests evolve, perhaps putting a greater emphasis on education or healthcare or another cause at any given moment. Those allocations will even be readily available on client-centric money management platforms that will supersede banking websites in providing a full-spectrum view of short-term saving, retirement, and charity spending for individuals. Donating will become as much a day-to-day norm as saving or spending is today, and it will extend much farther because giving will become enfolded into the act of paying. Today, some banks allow you to round up transaction payments and sweep the difference to a savings account. In the new paradigm, the same sweep will be seamlessly directed to your portfolio of charity organizations.

The availability of research data constitutes an important aspect of this vision. Data by itself is meaningless. If I tell you that a charity that two months ago served 12,000 meals is now serving 100 more, you cannot determine why this change has taken place, or even whether it's a good thing altogether. There needs to be context. Perhaps the charity has expanded its geographic scope, or perhaps grassroots campaigning has reached new ears. Perhaps it's a seasonal trend. Perhaps there are 100,000 hungry men, women, and children in that area and an extra 100 more meals is barely a dent in the curve.

A new paradigm will require research and analysis on a scale we have never imagined before, but thanks to the limitless capacity of cloud-based computing and the emergence of artificial intelligence, technology will supply it, and the philanthropic sector must embrace it. That research will not be limited to short-term output analysis but will extend to the tracing of nonprofit organizations' adherence to their prospective trajectories. Once a strategic plan is translated into measurable objectives, then the monitoring of outcomes and the measure of impact can begin and feed back to the donors.

In the same way that nowadays anyone can be an investor with the assistance of a broker to provide research and advice on financial undertakings, the new paradigm of philanthropy will make everyone a potential donor with professional intermediaries to provide relevant data and trustworthy counsel.

If everyone can give as seamlessly as they spend, and if everyone can trust as readily as they transact, then we can truly make fundraising transparent. However, this requires social innovation on an unprecedented scale.

To effectively address social problems, we must concentrate resources on solutions with proven efficiency. To do this, we must in turn identify the initiatives and programs that truly make a difference. The nonprofit world is not homogenous, and most donors do not know which organizations will get the job done. All nonprofits will do their best to earn good publicity in order to ensure fundraising success: few will report on failures, and even fewer on failures built on donor money. Nonprofits are held to higher standards than regular businesses because we expect them to be virtuous, driven only by their mission and not by a need to pay employees or grow their operations. Nevertheless, if we want to truly break down the barriers that prevent the timely resolution of social issues, we need to accept that current solutions have either run their course or shown their limits, that new solutions will only come from social innovation, and that while some of them will fail, most are worth trying.

We need to cut nonprofits some slack. We need to let them try to innovate, fail, and learn from their mistakes; this change in attitude will allow for increased transparency and hopefully increased innovation. Furthermore, when we find ones that work, we need to help them grow, identify why they work, and scale them to replicate the model wherever it is needed. But all that work requires a whole lot of knowledge that most donors do not have and have no time to acquire. As a result, the new paradigm will see the emergence of specialized intermediaries who will provide those services in a systematic and reliable way. Those specialists who make up the "Find, Fund, and Scale" pillar of the new philanthropy will also heavily rely on technology similar to that on the fundraising side. Much of this technology has not been invented—but it soon will be.

This is a new a paradigm that combines pervasive giving with focused resource allocation and meaningful social innovation.

We have solutions. All we have to do is implement them.

8

# Problem, Power, Pathway

"Change your life today. Don't gamble on
the future, act now, without delay."

—SIMONE DE BEAUVOIR

Timing is everything. The essence of good timing is to hit PLAY a fraction of a second before the rest of the world does. You have to choose the precise moment when your idea is ready to hatch—when society will welcome it with open arms—but before it exists anywhere else. Good timing also means accepting that people might laugh in your face, that they will call you a dreamer, a megalomaniac. People laughed in my face when, at twenty-two, I told them that the Minitel system in France was dying and would soon be replaced by the internet. They laughed in my face five years later when I bet everything on cell phones. These experiences helped me develop acumen and steeled me against mockery. They also taught me that timing acts as a compass that can help guide a business as it launches and expands.

In 2011 I was living in New York with my family and running two start-ups when I decided it was time for me to keep the promise I had made to myself when I was young: to help other people. At that point, helping an old lady cross the road or giving a few dollars to a homeless person was the closest I had come to philanthropy.

All I had was my entrepreneurial instinct, so I decided to act as if I were setting up a business and begin with market research. I had no thought then of creating Epic. In fact, I had no idea what I wanted to create. I sent out dozens of emails to all sorts of people either active in or knowledgeable about this field: philanthropists, social entrepreneurs, and political leaders.

Matt Bannick was one of the people who responded. Once number two at eBay, Matt had chosen to devote himself to running the Omidyar Network, a philanthropic investment firm created by eBay founder Pierre Omidyar. I told Matt about my plans: digging wells, building schools, changing the world in small practical ways. Matt responded with a question as simple as it was incongruous: "How many people can do that?" He gave me a week to think about it. The truth was, many thousands of people can do it—and have done it. With his question, Matt had forced me to consider what unique impact *I* could have: how to optimize my talents to help the greatest number of people.

Every one of us has a talent, something unique, an asset that makes us stand out from the rest. For me it came down to my entrepreneurial skills and tech experience.

After my conversation with Matt, I began asking myself more questions. What precisely could I do differently? What could I improve upon? It's a fairly common line of questioning among entrepreneurs—after hearing some shiny elevator speech proposing "the Uber of pizza slices"—to ask, "So, practically, what problem do you solve? What's your solution to address it gainfully?" That's where the real discussion begins.

How do you achieve that level of precision? You need a framework to formalize it. You need to periodically review it to learn from any shortcomings and allow the parameters that enable it to evolve. Almost since the beginning of Epic, I've been in touch with Professor Julie Battilana, faculty chair of the Social Innovation and Change Initiative (SICI) at the Harvard Kennedy School, which she and her colleagues developed in 2016 to help individuals and groups navigate the challenges of initiating and implementing social change. At Harvard, Julie developed a framework that comprises three Ps: the Problem, the Person (or People), and the Pathway. Interestingly, this framework fell in line with how Epic grew and operated.

The first step of the three Ps is Problem: defining exactly what you're trying to solve. There is virtually no chance for social entrepreneurs to successfully resolve a problem if they have not defined it. Definition lays fertile soil for the growth of meaningful social innovation. For Epic, we locate the problem in the world's injustices and the solution in grassroots organizations already accomplishing effective work on the ground. Our goal is to act as a bridge between the two.

The author or authors of that definition of the problem form the second aspect of SICI's framework: Person (or People). These people will not ultimately be the only stakeholders, but they are the spark that lights the fire. From this vantage point, SICI's frame-work invites social innovators to analyze the motivations and per-spectives (perhaps even the biases) they bring to the table. It also urges an analysis of the sources of power available. Sources of power can be personal, positional, or relational—in other words, the power of who you are, what you do, and who you know.

At Epic we saw power as such an instrumental aspect of the People dimension that we revised the framework and made Power our second P. We did this partly to ensure the focus remains on the movement and not those behind it. Since I founded Epic, people have often identified it with me. While I wish Epic to be the story of the remainder of my life and legacy, Epic is a movement, not a man. Its momentum must build up beyond me or any other indi-vidual. Epic is an ecosystem of Persons—professionals and friends who volunteer their expertise and their networks to make it hap-pen. But it is more than Persons, it is the nexus of five powers:

1. The power of *money*. Because Epic is independently funded, we can ensure that every dime given to Epic goes to support the organizations in our portfolio.

2. The power of *media*. At first, I mainly promoted Epic with my own life story and tried to use my privilege to amplify the voices of NGOs and the people they served. Now their stories are the ones that are the most salient and important.

3. The power of *networks*. Beyond the media, we have access to a tremendous network of professionals—CEOs,

investors, artists, entrepreneurs, communication gurus, journalists, policy makers, film directors—willing to help. We have organized this cohort into chapters of Epic Ambassadors in San Francisco, Los Angeles, New York, London, Brussels, and Paris.

4. The power of *knowledge*. I mentioned earlier that social disruption is not a matter of overturning tables; it must be grounded in reality. I spent years researching the philanthropic world before I attempted to change anything. You must have knowledge and understanding in order to make systemic change. So at Epic, we spend a lot of time developing our knowledge of the sector, continuously conducting research trips and collecting data, and then applying decades of cumulative knowledge from in-house specialists to make sense of it.

5. The power of *innovation*. It is easy to have ideas, much harder to deliver on them. Innovation is the power to turn ideas into action. It requires constant and patient cultivation. For us, innovation comes through not only in our selection and monitoring processes, but also in the way we encourage people in our network to interact: for example, we created an app to feed impact data to donors and throw a bridge between donors and beneficiaries.

In my mind, it is the conjunction of these powers that place Epic in a unique position to deliver on its mission.

The third aspect of the framework is the Pathway. Once you have defined the problem, you need to establish a vehicle for delivering the solution—how to get where you're going.

At Epic, our basic pathway is clear: we believe that we can address the problem of injustice through giving. And once we have established that instrument of giving, everything else falls into place. We orchestrate all axes and solutions to support the pathway, and that pathway remains illuminated by the beacon of the problem.

Guided by these three Ps, and after three years of research and hundreds of meetings with people who were already giving part of their resources to others, the first glimmers of Epic began to take shape. Now Julie's team at Harvard is writing up a case study on Epic. As they interview my staff and track our progress, I've benefited from the extra level of analysis and challenges to our assumptions. This productive exchange of feedback has helped Epic grow and kept our minds and perspectives open. The ultimate goal is to refine our model to the point that it can be readily replicable, letting giving reach anyone and everyone.

I had spent twenty years trying to bring innovation to various sectors. Now I would take on one of the oldest industries in the world—charity—and I would innovate. I knew that if I could address the concerns raised by the people I had met, I could meet a genuine need in society. When I did launch Epic, three essential conditions had fallen into place: a good idea, a good team, and perfect timing. A few years on, all we need is for others to join us in revolutionizing the way we give.

# 9

# Learning from People on the Ground

"The world is a book, and those who
do not travel read only a page."
—SAINT AUGUSTINE

In 2013 I sold my companies and set off on a journey around the world with my wife, Florence, and our three young kids. Everywhere we went we made sure to respectfully integrate and communicate with locals. We wanted to earn their trust and learn from them.

Every day I met with leaders of charities, philanthropists, social entrepreneurs, and politicians, but I also conversed with NGO workers on the ground and locals supporting their communities. In the morning I might be in the slums with my family, then in the evening sharing a meal with investors in a fancy restaurant. I learned as much from the former as from the latter.

In Hong Kong I learned that 2.5 billion people—almost one-third of the earth's population—do not have access to glasses that would fix their eyesight. James Chan, a member of the Synergos nonprofit network who served as our guide for a day, is obsessed with this subject. The heir to a family of industrialists, he was marked by his experience in Nigeria, where he was born and spent the first years of his life. As an adult, he chose to contribute to the development of the world by helping its inhabitants to see better. His start-up, Clearly, sells glasses, but that is not all it does: it operates on the principle of "buy one, give one"—for every pair of glasses purchased, one is donated by the company. In Rwanda alone, his foundation has trained two thousand nurses and sent representatives to free clinics in even the most remote small towns and villages to conduct eye exams and distribute glasses or, if necessary, book them an appointment with an ophthalmologist.

In Chiang Mai, Thailand, I learned about the tragedy of the children of immigrant workers who arrive from poorer countries such as Burma and Laos, and who survive in desperate conditions with their families, unable to speak the language of their new country. Magali Crosta, an extraordinarily good-hearted social worker, has founded an NGO, Baan Dek, which helps these children by giving them access to education—in other words, offering them a future. She took us to schools where we saw those children learning with newfound smiles.

In Ulaanbaatar, the capital of Mongolia and one of the world's most polluted cities, I witnessed an amusing incident while we were dining with the Mongolian minister of ecology. She and my wife and I had our kids with us, and they were all about the same age. Despite the language difference, they spent the whole evening in discussion. The ability children have to communicate, breaking through the barriers of verbal language, never ceases to amaze me.

In the United States, I met Bill Drayton, who is not only a social entrepreneur but the man who invented the concept. This was in the 1970s, just before he founded Ashoka, a gigantic network of social entrepreneurs who develop innovative methods of wealth creation. Ashoka's credo immediately won me over: "everyone is a changemaker." Without question, Drayton has changed the world. Every year he oversees projects that not only make the world a more fair place, but actually transform structures and mentalities to help each person discover the resources necessary to move forward.

Our tour of the world was, for me, another way of completing my market research. Wherever I went, the needs I found were immense, but so was the will to meet them. I realized that instead of trying to start another NGO or foundation focused on solving one specific problem, it would be more helpful to support organizations already successfully serving their communities.

# 10

# Design Thinking

"I remind myself every morning:
Nothing I say this day will teach me anything.
So if I'm going to learn, I must do it by listening."

—LARRY KING

"Design thinking" is the most efficient way of looking at a problem and finding a new angle. It goes against the classic vision we have of the brilliant inventor tinkering in his office or his garage and, without ever leaving his desk, discovering the keys to the success of a start-up which will, of course, soon become a "unicorn" company—valued at over $1 billion.

Design thinking is an entirely different way of operating. It works on the principle that no matter the qualities of the people sitting in a room and seeking a solution there, they will not find it for the simple reason that the solution exists beyond the room. In other words, you must go out into the world to find it, examine it, and build it in conjunction with the people for whom it is intended—i.e., the consumers—and look at it from their point of view.

Steve Jobs did this, and he brought people the solutions they needed even if, to start with, they weren't aware that they needed them. At the start of his entrepreneurial career, he even used IDEO, a consulting firm and one of the biggest purveyors of design thinking. Jobs faced a problem: how could users of his first computer—the Lisa, forerunner of the Mac—interact with the screen through their keyboard without too many complications?

The design thinkers of IDEO did not retreat into the countryside to think about this. On the contrary, they went into the streets, visited universities and businesses, and met dozens, hundreds of potential users and asked them: "What do you plan to do with this object?" Back in their laboratories, they created a product, tested it, and kept working on it until they had found a solution. And thus was born the mouse, the little tool that revolutionized the world of computing.

Talk to your audience. It may sound obvious, but I've known countless very smart leaders who failed to do so. A friend of mine once had a generous and theoretically brilliant idea: send thousands of tablets to children and adolescents in African villages to connect them to the world and perhaps, later, facilitate educational programs for them. But my friend did not speak with his consumers, the intended recipients of the gift. The result: disappointment on the part of these African villagers when they opened the boxes and found tablets, because their villages did not have access to electricity.

In theory, design thinking constitutes a multidisciplinary approach to problem-solving. Or, put more simply, it means looking at and resolving a problem from the point of view of the consumer. Most of the start-ups that succeeded, like Facebook or Google, operated in this fashion. Their creators had an idea, a desire, a problem; as the first users, each sought to resolve the problem in what seemed the most efficient way possible for other users.

Epic was born partly from design thinking. The three years that I devoted to market research enabled me to spot a need, and to specify and refine what I offered in response. I began with complicated subjects—fighting injustice and inequality, changing the system, changing the mentality around donations—but ultimately I had to propose solutions that were simple.

My starting point was not ideal: I stood between two worlds that struggled to communicate with each other. On one hand, people with huge financial resources, and on the other a shapeless mass of social enterprises and NGOs. As I questioned both sides, I came to realize that the lack of communication resulted from a persistent stereotype that could not be swept away overnight: those who had succeeded and earned a lot of money in the private sector were convinced that the leaders of social enterprises were dilettantes on a road to nowhere, people who were probably very nice but lacking any real skills, to whom they felt compelled to condescend: "Let me show you how it's done."

Now, these enterprises were often run by brilliant business-people, just as highly qualified and skilled as their private-sector counterparts. Nevertheless, this stereotype held strong and resulted in one-sided interactions, in which the NGOs—who needed the private-sector money to continue existing—hid behind a polite silence. There was no exchange, no reciprocal input that might have benefitted both parties.

Therefore, we made it our first mission to explain to those in the private sector why they ought to give. To show the intolerable needs that exist in the world and the impossibility, post-internet, of accepting a two-speed society with all its attendant injustices. To take a critical look at the sterile accumulation of wealth. We point to the frustration of young people culminating in mass movements like Occupy Wall Street and the mass poverty that can no longer be hidden. In these circumstances, sharing becomes a duty. What does it matter whether you make another one million or two million or five million when you have already accumulated more wealth than the world has ever seen before? Why, in such circumstances, would you not give? Or give so little?

A pitfall emerged in my discussions with donors: the lack of trust that comes with an avalanche of options. Scientific studies have shown that when you have more than seven options, you are more likely to procrastinate and make no choice at all. Our second mission then appeared clear to me: establishing selection criteria for the social enterprises that would constitute Epic's portfolio and funding those which would have a quantifiable social impact. This condition would increase the confidence of donors.

The methodology of design thinking led us to meet with hundreds of NGOs, foundations, and think tanks to listen to their requests and requirements. We established an initial application process that enables us to quickly analyze a social enterprise's structure and impact through a series of simple, clearly worded questions. We submitted our questionnaire to various organizations, reworked the questions in light of their responses, and ultimately came up with a document that can be filled out in forty-five minutes but contains enough information for us to carry out the preliminary groundwork.

# 11

# Keep an Open Mind

"It is a narrow mind which cannot look at a
subject from various points of view."

—GEORGE ELIOT

In parallel with design thinking, I have always based my projects around the concept of "open innovation."

Henry Chesbrough, a Berkeley professor, coined this term in the early 2000s to describe the flow of knowledge from external and internal sources that enriches a company's creativity and its capacity to innovate. Open innovation is made of three elements: the sharing of information, cooperation among companies, and trust.

Breaking with the culture of secrecy that prevailed in many sectors, the concept of open innovation quickly demonstrated its brilliance. Its popularity has now grown in conventional sectors in addition to the start-up world; NASA, among others, has started using it to resolve a number of problems, including specialized technical questions about progress in space exploration.

We can apply open innovation to every stage of the creative process, always with the same basic principle: opening oneself up to new horizons instead of hunkering down alone. Open innovation has us meeting new people, discussing common issues, breaking down barriers, sharing best practices, and daring to think laterally and to propose out-of-the-box ideas.

We can implement open innovation as soon as an idea emerges. I could not have developed Epic without it: I had to listen to experts on the ground and learn what they needed. I had to communicate their ideas and needs to companies with resources. Not knowing what I wanted, I had everything to learn. I opened myself up to any possibilities that might improve my idea, any innovations that might increase its effectiveness. It's an ambitious project. I experience creating and running Epic as an entrepreneurial adventure. Epic is a start-up, with almost all the characteristics of a start-up: testing ideas, keeping the ones with potential, and using them to find new ideas, new angles and approaches to adapt to the market. But unlike other start-ups, Epic has no business model. Our goal isn't profit. Our goal is to join the movement to make giving a normal, natural, and uncomplicated way of life.

We found ourselves with an assembly of ideas both impressive and eclectic. From Hollywood we had taken the possibility of 3-D and virtual-reality images. From Silicon Valley we took big data, algorithms, and the development of ingenious applications. We were inspired by Europe and its culture of partnerships. The big foundations inspired us with their selection processes, perhaps too complicated for our purposes, but ripe for adjustment and improvement.

We were looking to create Philanthropy 3.0, not just an initiative based on noble emotions and good intentions but one that would shatter the idealized image of the poor, self-sacrificing Good Samaritan. To achieve this, we needed to consult every possible source of insight and support. This input from others formed the lifeblood of the project.

# 12

# Always Ask Broad Questions

"Never doubt that a small group of thoughtful,
committed citizens can change the world.
Indeed, it is the only thing that ever has."

—MARGARET MEAD

Market research, design thinking, open innovation—all these concepts demand an open mind. People sometimes have a distorted view of what it means to implement an idea: they expect mountains of data, surveys, focus groups, and economic models. Many people have an attachment to data not based in a real-world context. Many marketers approach their research with preconceptions and shape their research questions to justify them: they test a model. Seldom do we hear about genuine research that makes no assumptions, that asks questions without knowing or expecting specific answers. And yet you can only succeed in challenging fundamental human behaviors if you approach them with an open mind. Ask broad questions, and ask them broadly.

I met with social innovators, with foundation executives, with NGO leaders and social entrepreneurs, and I asked them, "What do you need?" It takes time to ask the same question to hundreds of people around the world, but I received pretty consistent answers that helped me envision the nature of Epic's activities. For a start, I learned about the need for unrestricted grants, a fundamental aspect of giving that contributes to the most effective "strategic" philanthropy.

When someone makes a donation, they can either direct the funds to a specific project or program—the building of a new hospital wing, the funding of an immunization campaign, or the purchase of tablets for a classroom—or they can make their gift "unrestricted." When a gift is unrestricted, the money can be used for anything—from paying the staff of an organization to purchasing a truck or even launch a marketing campaign. We may perceive a directed donation as having a bigger impact (look—this is the hospital wing the money helped build, here are the tablets we purchased); because it's tangible, it reassures the donor. And yet, when I spoke with NGOs, they overwhelmingly voiced a preference for unrestricted donations. As they scale, social organizations need to invest in new projects, new staff, and new equipment in a nonlinear and sometimes intangible way, but ultimately this type of grant better enables them to achieve the big picture. After hearing the same answer again and again, we decided that any funds we'd distribute in the future would be unrestricted.

My second question was just as vague as my first one: "What else do you need to succeed?" As before, a remarkably consistent answer emerged: "We need multi-year funding."

Disruption takes time. Social innovation cannot be deployed in a single season, nor should we expect to succeed the first time around. Yet philanthropy has cornered itself into a situation in which donors expect a quasi-annual bulletin of good news and may even withhold funds from those that fail to publicize all the good they have achieved. As a result, philanthropy remains tactical. Programs that may take years to build up are shunned. Philanthropy rarely welcomes risk, and the prospect of a steady stream of donations over multiple years becomes less likely. The social entrepreneurs I consulted made it clear to me that if we want to support social innovation, we need that multi-year commitment. So I resolved that we would commit to support social innovators for the long haul.

I asked many other questions, from how to define a social impact trajectory to how to engage donors with the NGOs. After meeting with so many entrepreneurs, the potential contours of a disruptive approach became clearer. Another notion emerged: many social workers, nonprofit executives, strategists, program managers, and development officers have a deep, insightful, evolved understanding of the mission they pursue, and most of them believe passionately in their work. If we aim to reinvent philanthropy, we must listen to them. They know best how to do their work. We must work with them to ensure that they can articulate and convey their impact, and to empower them to deliver on their missions.

Everywhere I went I also spoke with donors. With them I also asked simple questions, centered on my perception that they felt unsatisfied with their own giving. "What's holding you back from giving more?" Their answers converged toward three main notions: that they did not trust nonprofits, that they did not know whom to give to, and did not have the time to investigate. As I dug further into those discussions, I understood the link between transparency and trust in terms of financial flow, but also in the measurement and articulation of impact. I knew Epic had to vet organizations intensely and report the impact of every donation. That way donors could rest assured that they were actually, and directly, supporting the causes they cared about.

I also realized through my questions that time presented a huge obstacle not only in conducting research on charities but in the act of donating. It's easy to put off donating money or registering to volunteer, thus my focus on promoting payroll giving and transactional giving. Philanthropy needs to find its place in the landscape of everyday people: it needs to use the same tools they use, to live where they live, to offer solutions embedded in their daily lives. Payroll and transactional giving exemplify painless, automatic, and systemic solutions for people lacking in time but willing to donate.

By the time I finished my market research, I had settled on a goal: to make giving the new norm. Everyone can be a philanthropist; this is not just the domain of the rich. How could we engage a young college student, or someone just starting an entry-level job? How could the average middle-class person become a strategic philanthropist, contribute to the fight against injustice, and perceive their impact?

When we initially launched Epic, we naturally targeted men and women already invested in philanthropic activities, not only because they would likely respond more readily to our innovations, but also because we wanted to test our approach in that existing, albeit imperfect, market. Soon, however, we attempted to open up our solutions to a mainstream audience through an initiative we named Epic Generation.

As the project progressed, we soon realized it wasn't the right approach. Our first problem was that we focused too much on selling Epic rather than offering people solutions. I spent hours trying to shrink our mission to six-second web banners. Instead of talking about the issues, we were just advertising ourselves.

So we changed course. After all, the true goal of Epic went beyond increasing our fundraising. We didn't need to convince people to fight injustice or donate to causes. They already had that appetite. We needed to bring them new and practical means of satisfying it. Furthermore, we needed to set an example others would emulate—that's why we used an open-sourced methodology from the start. So we moved toward finding ways for everyday people to give more—not only to Epic, but to give more in general. That's why we don't have a business model. In the end, we came to redefine what "Epic Generation" meant: rather than an entire generation giving to Epic, an entire generation of philanthropists on a mission to eliminate injustice by supporting impactful social innovations.

# 13

# Ensuring Lasting Impact

"The best way to not feel hopeless is to get up and do
something. Don't wait for good things to happen to you.
If you go out and make some good things happen, you will
fill the world with hope, you will fill yourself with hope."

—BARACK OBAMA

Epic soon required a platform that could meet all the needs of
everyone who donated. We came up with multiple methods of
donating, irrespective of the amount given. Our next mission
was to discover exceptional social enterprises. In order to meet
our donors' desires, we also enlarged the filter for enterprises we
selected to cover a broader spectrum of society's problems. In the
future, I have no doubt that we will continue to add new social
issues to our portfolio.

We should avoid falling into the trap of sentimental philanthropy. By that I mean the generous but ineffective paternalistic
practices of the past, which consisted in spreading one's resources
too thinly over a multitude of charities, of giving money to every

virtuous person with a begging bowl, without ever seeking to find out more about them. I'll admit that I've done this before. But we should not partake in inefficient and selfish giving. We don't have time for it. We must help people in a way that is real, high-quality, and sustainable.

In this world of endless choices—abundant enough to paralyze—we see hundreds of thousands of charities devoted to young people. And like tens of thousands of donors, I struggled at first to choose where to donate. So, with my team, I used design thinking to solve this problem, implementing an NGO selection process that would win our donors' trust. Donations will have a greater effect for all parties if they go to organizations with real impact. This is not unfair; it is efficient.

Selection does not imply judgement or criticism. It simply means choosing NGOs whose actions can be developed, transplanted, and replicated. Our process is not a lottery, but a selection of initiatives that fit into an overall plan: these organizations affect not only the lives of individuals but also address the broader challenge of running of a community. They know how to approach and resolve problems. They have programs that work, based on methods that can be applied to other areas. True, these criteria exclude very small charities in favor of more structured social enterprises, but this choice is deliberate: we do not want to gamble on microstructures that might grow one day but will most often remain limited to local impact, and perhaps even founder completely when the goodwill of their founders blows itself out.

For the same reason, we chose to partner with major organizations that have been working on the ground for years, such as the Fondation Bettencourt-Schueller in France, the Dasra foundation in India, the Segal Family Foundation in Africa, and Robin Hood in the United States. Each year, highly experienced organizations like these recommend to us the nonprofits they consider especially remarkable. We invite them to apply for support from Epic. We do the same thing with the NGOs our teams discover as they roam the planet. We also receive queries from a growing number of external applicants.

We give equal consideration to all of these applications, regardless of how they came to us. In 2018, the 4,000 dossiers we analyzed—and that figure rises every year—all went through the same selection process. We have settled on forty-five selection criteria to assess the social impact of each company, the quality of its management, and its method of operation. In an attempt to remain objective, we use an algorithm to scan and grade the dossiers. I am not a fan of delegating all tasks to machines, but if used wisely, I do believe they can help perform certain work more quickly and efficiently. I also think that at this stage of the selection process, identical criteria for all applicants makes for fairer evaluation. Human subjectivity and personal judgment tend, however involuntarily, toward some form of unfairness.

Having said that, the human element remains: our teams check the algorithms' selection, then follow through with the process, weeding out most of the dossiers to keep only the best: fewer than forty applicants. We then go out to meet these finalists on the ground, wherever in the world they happen to work, eventually selecting ten or so nonprofits to support.

While every choice comes with an element of risk, the selectivity and transparency of the process allows us to win the trust of the individuals and companies who give the money to support these social organizations.

We keep the chosen NGOs in our selection pool for at least three years. We pass on all the money that we collect on their behalf, but in exchange we ask for cooperation with our transparency reporting. We observe them, monitor their work, expect regular reports, interview them methodically every quarter, and go to visit them on the ground. This allows both the donors to see the achievements of their collective impact—what has changed as a result of their donation: the number of beds added thanks to their money, the training or activities they have financed, the teachers who have benefitted from their generosity, the qualifications obtained by students. And this also gives the nonprofits valuable information and analysis on their work: they can then use this data to see what they do well and where they can improve.

Through Epic, I've had the joy of seeing donors and nonprofits work together to amplify impact. Simplon, a network of programmers, developers, and web designers cofounded in 2013 by Frédéric Bardeau and his team, offers free seven-month training programs to anyone willing to learn, from senior citizens to refugees to the long-term unemployed. Beyond the world of computing, Simplon also helps students with public speaking and interviewing skills, giving them all the necessary tools to find employment on their own.

Simplon is run through a franchising system: public or private donors can create a school in response to the needs of their community. Septodont, a medical supply company based in the suburbs of Paris, became interested in funding Simplon. Septodont had started out as an Epic donor. But after a year, they approached us about getting involved more directly. Eventually Septodont and Simplon worked together to fund a computing school. The project merged Simplon's community network and teaching resources with Septodont's resources and job opportunities. Our teams facilitated the financial and legal arrangements with local bodies: the Saint-Maur mayor's office provided premises adjacent to Septodont's headquarters; Saint-Maur Entreprendre, a network of entrepreneurs, also joined the movement. Septodont agreed to take part in the training programs, making its computers available and organizing master classes where its employees would teach the students.

In October 2017, Val-de-Marne inaugurated its first social school for computing in the presence of the town's mayor and the employment minister along with fifteen students from the most disadvantaged areas of the town. It was the perfect marriage of social entrepreneurship and the common good.

We acknowledge that in most cases donors want to support causes they truly care about and are hungry to explore the outcome of their philanthropy. By giving them these tools, they can become more involved and truly understand the issues at hand. Transparency helps humanize everyone involved.

# 14

# Give Time. Give Expertise.

"No one is useless in this world who
lightens the burdens of another."
—CHARLES DICKENS

Not everyone can donate money, but that does not preclude the ability to enact social change. Each and every one of us has skills and time we can use to make an impact.

When my family and I moved to Brooklyn in 2010, we enrolled our kids in the local public schools, and while cheering from the bleachers and juggling sleepovers we befriended the parents of our children's friends: the Herringtons.

A proud child of New Orleans, T.G. Herrington grew up in a remarkable family. His parents had felt the urge to reach out to some local populations deprived of access to healthcare in Latin America. T.G.'s father worked in the import/export business and first identified the need. When he passed away at a very young age, his wife took over the challenge and worked painstakingly to build an outreach network. After founding an orphanage in Honduras, T.G.'s mother invited physicians and healthcare professionals to visit them all over Latin America and experience firsthand the impact they could have in delivering and administering medicines and care to regions without access to modern medicine. During his early years in Panamá, Nicaragua, El Salvador, Honduras, Guatemala, Argentina, and Colombia, T.G. witnessed both injustice and the ability of individuals to make a difference. He also saw those doctors returning again and again because they could nurture a tangible, compelling sense of impact.

T.G. spent his formative years learning the art of film and video editing. From ads to music videos, he worked with nationwide and global brands, including a Pepsi ad for the Super Bowl. He even collaborated on music videos for Michael Jackson. When the adventure of Epic began to take shape, T.G. felt naturally drawn to contribute, but instead of making a monetary donation, he gave something more valuable: expertise. He decided that each year he would donate two months of his time to record and capture photos and movies for Epic.

I knew when I founded Epic that communication would be a pillar of our work: it was necessary for our advocacy and to connect donors and beneficiaries. Nonprofit communication brings numerous challenges, starting with the need to secure authentic and accurate depictions of the needs of the people we help with dignity—without sinking into condescension. Working with organizations that help children and youth, we found ourselves with the even more delicate task of reporting on injustices toward children without compromising their protection. That delicate balance that aims to shield more than expose, and inform more than describe, was precisely what T.G.'s professional experience could bring.

T.G. came on board during our very first selection trip. Over the course of these four years, T.G. has perfected the art of losing himself to find others. His approach undoubtedly possesses an epic dimension that allows him to relinquish control of the circumstances and to allow the people and the location to rise and shape the story. To capture the authenticity of happenstance, the unscripted essence of a moment, you need to open more than the shutter of your camera: you need to reach the stillness of your soul and let your heart meander. Then the stories you bring back speak to the hearts of others. That's the gift T.G. brought us.

As we progressed in our exploration of impact, T.G. forayed into new territories: he pioneered the use of virtual reality to transport donors to the very location where their money turns to outcomes. He went to interview donors and beneficiaries, ambassadors and social entrepreneurs who could all contribute to the discussion around Epic. He has helped us turn our mission into pictures that speak a thousand words.

I realized that Epic was truly lifting off when impressive people I had never met took an interest in helping us. In 2015, I met Hope Solo. We were both in Bangkok, participating in the One Young World summit. Naturally, I had heard of this incredible soccer player before: a celebrity in the United States, a formidable goalkeeper, nicknamed "the 202-game player" (she had played 202 games on a national team). She had just taken home the Women's World Cup after winning the Olympic gold medal two times in a row, in 2008 and 2012. Obviously, we started out talking about soccer. I played club soccer for several years, and I now coach my daughter Alice, which Hope found amusing. At the time, Epic was just taking shape, and Hope was excited about the idea. She later came to visit our offices in New York.

Hope Solo has been a longtime champion of equality between male and female soccer players. When we met, she was planning to threaten a boycott of the Olympics in Rio if female soccer players continued to receive less payment than their male counterparts. She has also thrown herself into another battle—to make soccer accessible to all children and not just, as she put it, to "rich white kids" whose parents can afford club registration fees and travel to tournaments.

Hope Solo asked me how she could help us and she was thrilled with the solution we came up with: she could give us an hour of her time, put her goalkeeper's uniform back on and face up against . . . an Epic donor. Sold at auction, this single hour netted $10,000!

Of course, you don't have to be a world champion to make a tangible impact with your skills. Everyone has something to contribute. Ask yourself, "What is my greatest skill? How can I share that ability?" Maybe you are very good at explaining difficult concepts in grammar or math. Look for an opportunity as a tutor at a local public school. Maybe you're artistic. See if you can help local nonprofits by photographing events or making posters. Everyone has the ability to contribute. You just need to find your own best way of doing so.

# 15

# Easy Giving

"For it is in giving that we receive."
—FRANCIS OF ASSISI

My experience with Epic has proven that, when presented with a painless platform for giving, even the most unlikely of companies will jump on board. My relationship with Dior began this way: a brief meeting with the company's HR head, a desire to take the exchange further, a meeting with the company's employees, a scheduled speech. It was May, the first day of good weather in Paris that spring. Given the choice between 80°F sunshine after weeks of cold and rain and a speech about the necessity of giving away your money, most people in my generation would undoubtedly have opted for the former. But every seat in the room was taken: young people, middle-aged people, men, women.

The HR head and I had developed ideas together. For months, she had wanted to bring a more human element to the company's social responsibility policy. She had noticed a real urge among the company's employees toward social commitment, a desire to participate in something bigger than their own lives and careers, to have a positive impact on the world, on society, on the environment. This desire shone through in job interviews where, for a few years now, these topics had kept recurring, with the applicants more concerned about Dior's social impact than their chances of being issued the latest smartphone. The HR head also noted a very positive reaction from employees when the company made public its commitment to improving its impact on society.

Together, we examined various solutions. Dior wanted to immediately implement payroll giving and match employee donations with its own donations: that way, giving would become a unifying force between employers and employees, a connection between two parties in search of a shared commitment.

The company organized a vote to decide on the recipients. They chose to support M'Lop Tapang's work with refugee children in Cambodia and SNEHA's mission to empower women in India. A few months later, 20 percent of the employees had opted for payroll giving. These employees worked in many different departments, were of various ages, and were not all well-paid: a janitor was just as likely to give as a senior executive.

I might as easily use the example of Derichebourg. With 34,000 mostly blue-collar employees in fourteen countries and $3.1 billion in revenues, the company implemented payroll giving at the urging of its CEO Boris Derichebourg. The employees voted in favor of three nonprofits, two of them—Sport dans la Ville (Sport in the City) and Simplon—supported by Epic.

Whether in the luxury goods or the public transport sector, whether most of their employees are executives or laborers, these companies act on identical motivations: not only to meet the requirements of their corporate social responsibility policy, but also to keep their employees—who, they have realized, are just as likely to leave them out of a need for purpose as for a competitive position or a higher salary.

The system has changed. For the older generation, this can be disorienting. But let's not forget, the arrival of electricity disoriented the older generation of the time, as did the arrival of the internet. Then people came to terms with the change and it became an integral part of their lives. The same will happen with giving. Soon, giving money to charity will be no more remarkable than turning on a lamp.

16

# How Much Giving Is Enough?

"We can never judge the lives of others, because each
person knows only their own pain and renunciation."

—PAULO COELHO

I confess that I often "judge a book by its cover." I try to reason with myself: who am I to judge whether what you give is sufficient? I know that we have not all benefited from the same upbringing, that we haven't been taught the same things, that it is not my place to define right and wrong, that some people's lives give them a deep-rooted, visceral fear of not having enough money.

In 2010, Bill Gates and Warren Buffett launched the Giving Pledge, a campaign targeted exclusively at the ultrarich: all those who sign up promise to give at least half of their fortunes to social causes.

At first sight, this initiative seems extremely laudable. The world has more billionaires than ever before. In 2007, they totaled 946; ten years later, that figure had risen to 2,043. And never has each billionaire possessed so many billions: in 2017, their total fortune was more than $7,067 billion. By 2018, the campaign had signed up 173 pledgers, aged between thirty and ninety. These billionaires represent twenty-one different countries, although the majority are American.

Personally, I consider the Giving Pledge an extraordinary initiative. However, the cut-off figure of 50 percent goes against my personal philosophy of giving. In my opinion, it gives rise to judgment and stigmatization rather than encouragement and goodwill. Does someone who gives away 25 percent of their possessions not deserve our respect? No matter how much we give, it will never be enough, but I will continue to fight for my belief that giving should become something other—and more—than an obligation: a norm.

How much do you give? It doesn't matter to me. Just give—share what you can. Don't let yourself be intimidated, just follow your heart. Fifty percent? A half of a percent? You are the only arbiter of your capacity to change the world.

Unfortunately, not everyone I meet is a Bill Gates or Warren Buffett. I remember a California venture capitalist to whom I outlined Epic's objectives and who abruptly interrupted me saying: "I don't agree. I call that communism." He clearly meant the word as an insult. "If you believe that communism means sharing and working toward a more equal division of wealth," I replied, "then in that case, you're right—I'm a communist." I never saw that man again.

For me, Peggy Dulany represents the opposite end of the spectrum. Born a Rockefeller, Peggy uses her middle name to pursue her philanthropic endeavors unencumbered by prestige. After working as a teacher for disadvantaged youth in Massachusetts, she founded the Synergos Institute to reduce global poverty and developed the Global Philanthropists Circle. She has created a new legacy of her own through targeted and considerable philanthropy.

Most people I meet lie somewhere between that California venture capitalist and Peggy Dulany. I always tell them, "You should give and you should tell people that you give." Not to bask in the glory of your generosity, but to give extra value to your donation: to let it serve as an example. To make giving something that seems like a normal everyday thing.

I have had some of my most difficult and complicated conversations about giving with Fortune 500 companies, but convincing these large companies to give a share of their profits has become easier over time. Social responsibility has become a talent management concern and a customer retention priority—a corporate survival imperative. The development of corporate social responsibility programs stems from that realization. The perception of such developments as "social washing," the necessary ticking of a box rather than the product of sincere belief that it was the right thing to do, is still a rightful concern, but my view is more practical. If shame or publicity is what motivates a company to be more socially responsible, then we should take advantage of that while trying to push for an actual systemic mentality shift. We work with what we have while striving for our ideals.

I recently met the boss of a large corporation with annual profits of several billion euros: a formidable man, aware of the new realities of these times. He described his belief in the importance of companies' social responsibilities. I asked him for the figures: how much money did they give every year? He seemed surprised by the question and said he didn't know. He asked the woman in charge of CSR (corporate social responsibility) and when he found out the answer, seemed suddenly dismayed. The company gave $500,000 per year to social causes. The head of human resources joined our discussion, mentioning her frustration at the high turnover of young executives. Many had left not for higher salaries but to join nonprofits. She found it hard to understand this new phenomenon and admitted that her company was going to have to adapt.

I offered them one of Epic's solutions for boosting a company's social DNA: payroll giving. The HR head explained that she had considered this solution, but that the finance department had blocked it due to the $20,000 cost of installation. There and then I took out my checkbook and told them, "I'll give you that money." Of course, they did not accept it.

Have I softened my stance over the past few years? I am willing to grant mitigating circumstances to individuals: it is possible that they remain unsure, not about whether they should give, but about how and to whom they should give. I also understand that they would prefer to give nothing rather than give erroneously. For all these reasons, I have made it my mission to provide the tools that will help people to give more and better: empathy, solutions, and reasons to hope.

# 17

# A Virtuous Circle of Communication

"In charity there is no excess."

—FRANCIS BACON

Alain Cojean is a friend of mine. He recently sold the restaurant chain he founded in 2001—what he called his "baby." The sale broke his heart, but he told me he didn't have a choice. At fifty-six, he wanted to use the time left to him for something more important than business. He wanted to work on the most essential task of all: helping and giving, doing his share.

In fact, he had been doing his share for years, but in secret. His Cojean chain belonged to a holding company called Harpan—a Breton word that means to help, to give, to rescue, to redistribute. He saw the company as a sort of means of expression. His goal was never to become rich but to do the best he could: to create the best restaurant chain possible, to promote good products, to offer healthy eating options for city dwellers while ensuring a happy work environment and a share of the company's profits for his employees—an ethical project.

Right from the beginning—from the first euro the company earned—part of the profits went toward good causes. In Cojean's account books, the lines of "donation" gradually grew so numerous that his accountant urged him to streamline his generosity. Thus the Feed, Love, Give foundation came into being.

Projects sprouted from chance meetings. In 2010, for example, Alain Cojean was in Calcutta when he came across a center for disabled children abandoned by their parents. The center sheltered, fed, and loved them, but the children spent their days doing nothing but watching television.

The day of his departure, he drank tea with the children in a circle on the tile floor. Alain looked at the cookie tin at the middle of the circle, which the children would reach into for a treat now and again. He had an idea. He decided to create a cookie factory. He found a proper location, trained the young people in the center, and established a factory specializing in fruitcake, French delicacies such as *madeleines* and *financiers* and, more recently, the delicious Breton cookies known as *traou mad*. The cookie factory became a success and now supplies the four- and five-star hotels in the city, as well as various restaurants. The children have grown into young adults who regularly send him photographs of them holding up their paychecks like trophies. Alain replicated this project in Cambodia and has plans to expand the idea to other places, too. In fact, Alain Cojean has a plethora of projects—a school, a farm, a nutrition center—to which he now wishes to devote most of his time.

A few months ago, Alain would not have wanted me to mention him in these pages. A humble, discreet man, he always shunned the limelight. When a financial newspaper reported that he had distributed just over 50 percent of the net profit from the restaurant sale to his employees and foundation, Alain was upset. Then he read the words of another restaurant chain owner about to sell his business: "Cojean has screwed everything up. Now I'm going to look like a piece of shit if I don't do the same thing he did."

At last, Alain understood the virtuous potential of communication: the snowball effect. I have known of this for years. Some people accuse me of being too hungry for publicity—and I'll admit that they have a point. But I sincerely believe that *without* that publicity, Epic's message would have remained obscure. And that message urgently needs to be spread.

As for Alain, he is pursuing his dream: not just to feed the world, but to feed it *well*. He is aware that this dream will not come true in his lifetime, but he won't throw in the towel. He's doing all that he can.

# 18

# Rules for Painless Giving

"True generosity is an offering; given freely
and out of pure love. No strings attached.
No expectations. Time and love are the most
valuable possession you can share."

—SUZE ORMAN

Every day, people ask me the same question.

*How much should I give?*

Giving as I understand it, at least the kind of giving that most people will perform, must be painless—it should always bring happiness, not only to the recipient but to the giver as well. So this excludes all the ideas of sacrifice, hardship, bitterness, self-interrogation, and penitence to which centuries of Judeo-Christian morality have accustomed us. Furthermore, let us give, absolutely, but always from the fat, the surplus, always from our disposable income, in such a way that we hardly feel the loss. On these conditions, giving can develop one of its greatest virtues: while helping others, it creates a positive self-image in ourselves, a source of self-confidence and optimism for the future. We cease to benefit from this second virtue when we give more than we can afford.

Knowing how much to give requires each of us to do a little bit of work to determine what I call the "pain level" of the donation. This level varies according to each individual. Many factors determine it: culture, education, age, career prospects, family burdens, personal commitment. We don't need a mathematical formula to calculate this threshold; all we need to do is to take a step back and reflect on it. Giving should not be a punishment or a catharsis. Giving is a joy, a gift. It helps us realign with our natural altruism. It brings us back to our true nature. So how do you find the pain threshold? Start by giving a little on a regular basis and see if you feel the difference. Many of the solutions we promote at Epic exist in that zone of entirely painless giving.

Once you've become accustomed to giving a little bit, try to increase what you give. See how it goes. You should remain comfortable. Don't miss a mortgage payment and don't stop saving for college funds, retirement, or healthcare accounts: the sustainability of your livelihood depends on those in the long run. If at some point you start feeling that giving more would lead you to sacrifice something necessary, take it as a signal that you may have reached your pain threshold.

The rule is never to go beyond that level. In fact, it is best to stay slightly shy of it. If giving becomes painful (unless we will it so as a sacrifice) we will regret giving and won't do it again. Some will opt for a monthly sum—ten dollars or ten thousand, it doesn't matter, as long as this regular donation provides the giver with a feeling of joy. I like to suggest designating a percentage of income, as various religious institutions have done. In which case, should you give 2 percent? 10? Again, the actual figure doesn't matter, as long as it causes you no pain.

The pain level is not an invariable figure, even for one person: it can evolve, both with your finances and with the "happiness" factor. Giving always makes me happy, and in my experience the more one gives, the happier one feels and the more one wants to give as a result. The ten painless but happy dollars of today will still be painless tomorrow, but will they be enough to keep me happy? Perhaps I should consider upping my monthly donation to twelve or fifteen dollars?

Some people make the mistake of thinking that the pain level percentage for the very rich ought to be much higher than for ordinary mortals. They'll have plenty of money left anyway, right? But having more money does not make it easier to give 2 percent or 10. For the rich, as for the poor, that proportion represents a significant proportion of what they have. No matter who you are, it all comes down to trial and error and developing a balance over time.

# 19

# Success Stories

"You see, idealism detached from action is just
a dream. But idealism allied with pragmatism, with
rolling up your sleeves and making the world bend a
bit, is very exciting. It's very real. It's very strong."

—BONO

I built Epic on the premise that giving can remedy injustice by supporting social innovation, but this premise falls apart without the people driving that social innovation. As an entrepreneur, I have learned the hard way that growing a company takes sweat, sleepless nights, and never-ending work, but I knew after a few years that the business would become profitable and marketable and that I would exit it with a substantial payout. Nonprofit workers know the sweat and the sleepless nights, but they rarely get any recognition for the work they do. They act selflessly to eradicate the injustices that plague the people they serve. They are some of the finest women and men I have met. As we share the stories of generous business leaders, we should give even greater importance to the stories of the people on the ground.

## ALI FORNEY CENTER

These stories don't always come from the other side of the world. In fact, several of our organizations operate within the US, sometimes just blocks away from our offices.

At six years old, Gabrielle secretly borrowed her mother's lipstick. At eight, she tried on her clothes when her mother was out. At eleven, her mother caught her putting on makeup. Right away, she took her to church to pray. Gabrielle was supposed to be a little boy at the time, and her family informed her that she was possessed and would end up in Hell. She was brought to therapist after therapist and forced to pray for hours on end, all while being denounced as disgusting. None of it made a difference. She was who she was: a girl. At seventeen, doctors declared her schizophrenic because, despite all the praying, she still wasn't "cured." She began psychiatric treatment. A man who noticed her in her native North Carolina gave her some money to run away. She caught a bus and wound up in New York, living on the streets, in the snow, in a world of unimaginable cruelty. She almost died.

Every year in the United States, thousands of young LGBT+ identifying people, just like Gabrielle, run away from home or are kicked out of the house by their families. They leave their hometown and head for New York, which has the reputation of being a tolerant city and the one with the most job opportunities. Once there, they have to face the realities of an expensive and difficult city. With no money and nowhere to live, they join the ranks of the homeless: 40 percent of young homeless people in New York are LGBT, with an average age of 14.4 years old.

In 2002, the Ali Forney Center, a tiny six-bed shelter, opened in the basement of a church in Harlem to help these endangered children. In the first seventy-two hours after their arrival in the city, with nothing to eat and no means of getting warm, half of them had already been urged to prostitute themselves. The Center's founder, Carl Siciliano, named it after his friend Ali, a transgender New Yorker who started living on the street at age thirteen. He managed to survive only by dealing drugs, and he had a reputation with the police because he was brave enough to confront them, begging them not to turn a blind eye to all the transgender and homeless people neglected by law and society on the streets. When Ali was seventeen, he entered a homeless center run by Carl. The following year, Ali was murdered. Carl has continued to fight on his behalf.

The organization grew in size: along with a real emergency accommodation center and a clinic, it has also developed teaching and training programs and has funded apartments to shelter older teenagers. Not only does it give them a roof over their heads, the Ali Forney Center prepares these young people, as a real family would, to manage on their own and escape the welfare system. The NGO supports them during their studies or apprenticeships and helps them find work and build new lives. In this way, the Center's one-hundred-and-fifty-strong team of doctors, teachers, coaches, cooks, etc. helps 1,500 young people every year.

Gabrielle was spotted by one of the Center's teams and treated by their doctors. One morning, she was finally able to look at herself in the mirror. She burst out crying: "I didn't think I'd ever be beautiful again."

## KIRON

Even when operating a bit farther from the United States, organizations often address needs that echo concerns readily found at home. For instance, in Germany, where the refugee crisis has become a prominent concern, Kiron was founded to help young refugees gain professional training in a scalable manner through the use of virtual campuses and courses. It has 2,700 students enrolled in its online classes, and forty-seven partner universities (including MIT) in eight countries. It prepares its students to become engineers, IT professionals, economists, and social workers and offers degrees in political science, just like any other university.

Kiron's students had all seen their lives change irrevocably when they became refugees. Just as intelligent as anyone else, and perhaps even more motivated, they only lacked a pathway into the future: copies of identity papers and diplomas left behind when they fled their home countries, assistance overcoming language barriers, and the funds for tuition.

Kiron offers each student personalized guidance to get them as far as possible in their studies. Algorithms and mentors, an online help desk and student office—these all work in synergy to develop a career plan that will take into account a wide spectrum of variables, handicaps, and—most of all—assets. All these students require is a leg up into the stirrup; after that, they can ride perfectly well on their own.

After taking language classes, the students can take online courses that allow them to acquire skills and a degree, or—better still—to accumulate credits that will enable them to join a campus in a more conventional university. Kiron is doing more than just giving student lessons: Kiron is giving people a second chance and the opportunity to pursue a new life with the resources to succeed.

## PRERANA

Priti Patkar was twenty-two in 1986 when she founded Prerana. On a research trip for her master's degree in social work she went into Kamathipura—the city's red-light district—she came across a grandmother, her daughter, and granddaughter who were working the streets together. Around them was a swarm of children, aged only five or six, who drummed up business for their own mothers who waited for clients in the brothels nearby.

India has more than a million prostitutes, and 40 percent of them are under the age of eighteen. In villages, families sell off their little girls to survive. In cities, the girls often wind up in tiny cells with just their clothes, a few provisions, and a camping stove under the bed to share with another girl. They are forced to sell their bodies—anyone who refuses is locked in a wooden cage without food or water until they relent. They have no choice: they belong to their pimp and must work for ten to fifteen years to buy themselves out of their debt. And even then they stay, because they have nowhere else to go. Any children they conceive grow up in these cells. The boys learn to smuggle; at nine years old, a girl's virginity is sold for a high price. After that, the girls inevitably end up in the same line of work as their mothers.

When Priti founded Prerana on the outskirts of Kamathipura, the local mafia couldn't believe their luck. Without expecting anything in return, this NGO would educate the children, treat their injuries and illnesses, and transport them to school and back. As far as the pimps were concerned, the business plan was clear: the little girls would become high-class escort girls. But this was not Priti's plan. She was determined to offer these children a real chance. When the pimps realized this, they fought against her bitterly, sullied her reputation, and threatened her life. But by then it was too late: Prerana had gained support from the local authorities and prominent local civilians.

To this day, more than 10,000 children of prostitutes have spent several years in Prerana's centers. They have all gone to school, and a good number of them have studied at university too. A few have gone on to take MBA courses, and many have followed their dreams. And each one of those children, after landing a good job with a decent income, has had the same reflex: to rescue their mothers from Kamathipura.

## THE BRILLIANT CLUB

The Brilliant Club is an NGO founded by two British schoolteachers, Jonathan Sobczyk and Simon Coyle, who were fed up with the inequality of education they saw in their country. Despite lots of rhetoric about equal opportunity, they could see that, in their classes, it was not the most brilliant students who went to the best universities (Oxford, Cambridge, London School of Economics) but those from wealthier families, those who knew more about the complicated entrance procedures for those universities. And the others? Only one in fifty dared to apply, even though their grades and abilities should have marked them out for extraordinary careers.

The two teachers appealed to their friends, then to friends of friends—university lecturers, researchers, scientists—and they organized, at first on a very small scale, a tutoring program. In the first year, of the twelve children who joined the Brilliant Club, eight received offers of admission from those select universities.

The program quickly grew. In 2017 more than 10,000 kids with high potential but from low-income families benefited from this helping hand in the form of evening classes, work experience, and intensive courses. Volunteers talk about their passions to young people who have never visited a museum. They introduce the kids to doctors and astrophysicists who tell them about the value of their work. These children will be the next generation of doctors, engineers, researchers, scholars, and entrepreneurs—the job creators of tomorrow. Young graduates from those same universities who have trained to supervise them may well move into teaching work. A win-win for society and for social mobility.

# 20

# Purpose Is the New Currency

I often find myself impressed by the passion and dedication of younger generations. You are the "We Generation." We were the "Me Generation." You want to share, you want your lives to have a purpose. You care, you believe in relationships, generosity, and other people. You want to do good. My generation was too selfish: the heroes in our movies were killers and tough guys; greed was our god. We calculated our values in dollars.

I see you when I give speeches. You raise your hands, taking pictures with your phones of the screen behind me, where the words that have become our slogan are emblazoned: *Purpose is the new currency*.

Purpose works invisibly. Neither intelligence nor feeling drives it. It exists beyond thought; it is what you are. Caring for your loved ones and for people you don't even know. Caring about the planet that we have left to you in such a terrible state. Caring as a kind of second nature, your true nature.

You do not think in terms of helping: words such as "paternalist" and "colonialist" have no place in your vocabulary. You prefer simply to share, and rightly so. You do not give, you form partnerships. You do not perform acts of charity, you stand beside others in order to move forward with them.

You have deconstructed our social organization. At first we saw it as a joke. Then the world you imagined drew us in. Nowadays, when employers' organizations and investment banks ask me to tell them about sharing, about social causes, I know that you have won. I feel confident that once the older generations leave our little comfort zone and join you in the search for solutions, we will not slip back into the old ways.

Thanks to you, the dollar and the euro have lost their crown. Purpose is the new currency.

You can wield the power of the consumer, of the citizen, of the worker. Use it wisely. Show them that from now on, your consumption has value. Take a stance as a tax payer. Call out your bosses to demand social investment. Unsubscribe. Walk away. Delete the app. Agitation will arise in the C-suite with the click of a mouse or the tap of a screen.

You have the power to choose how to spend your time. Work for companies that embrace sharing. If you are an entrepreneur, take the leap and implement a giving program. When looking for a job, ask about corporate responsibility. They may give you a boilerplate answer. Then ask again and scratch the surface.

You have the power to give. Find the impactful organizations that you want to support. Engage with them. Embrace giving as a practical habit in your life. Love it. Rejoice in it. A little bit of it will change you from within. Sharing as a lifestyle will make you happy—and more, it will make you whole.

# A Guide to Effective Giving

If you are looking for ways to making giving a bigger part of your life and sharing that experience with others, here are materials for inspiration.

## TO HUMAN RESOURCES

*Here is an example of email you can send to your HR department to enquire about implementing payroll giving programs:*

Dear_____,

I hope everything is going well.

I've read our organization's corporate social responsibility policy and felt encouraged by our mission as I've been trying to find ways to give back to causes that I care about. I recently heard about a program called payroll giving. This program allows for employees to donate a percentage of their paycheck to a nonprofit. In many cases the employer will match that donation—like a 401(k) for charity. Many organizations offer this program, including UNICEF and the Epic Foundation.

I don't believe we have any such system in place and would be highly interested in having payroll giving as an option. I also think that many of my colleagues would appreciate more opportunities to help support the causes they care about. I would love to start a conversation about how we can implement this program and what I can do to help.

Thank you.

Sincerely,

_____

## AT JOB INTERVIEWS

*When you attend a job interview, you can ask one of the following questions. Carefully review the answer they provide for signs of genuine interest in social impact.*

- What does your company do to contribute to social innovation?
- How are your employees engaged in social initiatives?
- Have you implemented some give-back initiatives for the staff or the company?
- What is the social footprint of your company?

*If offered a job, regardless of whether you accept it, make sure to let the hiring manager know that the availability of social programs is a factor influencing your decision.*

## TO RETAILERS

*Small shops are where you are most likely to find the owners when you visit, but managers of larger retail stores are always interested in hearing feedback from clients too, so don't hesitate to ask to speak with them. Many retailers also have suggestion boxes or comment cards.*

*If you use a comment card or send an email, you can use the following language:*

I enjoyed my experience shopping at your store. However, I would love to see your business implement a system of transactional giving. For example, most of my purchases do not result in a round number. I would like to be given the option to round up to the next dollar and have the difference given to charity. Some stores offer this option during checkout. I feel a greater loyalty to those businesses and feel more satisfied about my purchases if I can do a good deed at check out. Please consider implementing transactional giving.

*If you are conversing face-to-face, you can ask the following questions:*

- Hello, who can I talk to about your store/company's social responsibility policy?
- What is your business's social responsibility policy? Does it include charitable giving options for clients?
- Do you give your clients the ability to round up their total to the next dollar and give the difference to charity?

If not, would you be interested in implementing such a transactional giving option?

## TO BUSINESS OWNERS

*If you would like to take the Epic Sharing Pledge, you can use the text below and send us a signed copy. The pledge is not legally binding so you do not need to have it reviewed by your counsel, although as with any financial decision, you may want to seek professional advice on it.*

Today, by taking this pledge I am joining a movement of business leaders, investors, entrepreneurs, and influencers working to change the world by embedding giving into their life's work. This letter will document our understanding regarding the pledge of _____(the "Donor") to pay ___% (_____ percent) of the Donor's after-tax annual profits for a period of _____ as a donation to the Epic Foundation portfolio (the "Beneficiary"). Donor's Pledge shall be made in the form of a donation to Epic Foundation. The parties wish to avoid the need for modification of existing operating agreements, contracts, partnership agreements, and other pre-existing arrangements in which you may have entered within the normal course of doing business. As such, this letter does not assign Epic Foundation or the Beneficiary a legal right in the form of any membership interest, guaranteed financial or non-financial donation, or other economic interest to the assets of the Donor.

# Acknowledgments

To Fabrice, my brother and guardian angel, who has constantly inspired me to question myself, I send all my love.

To my beloved parents, thank you for making me a lucky boy since the day I was born.

Infinite thanks to Djénane Kareh Tager and Max Colas, who listened and patiently helped me during this literary adventure, and also to Susanna Lea and to my editor Juan Mila.

To my Epic teams, in particular Nicola Crosta, Sam Giber, Myriam Vander Elst, Aude Anquetil, Max Colas, Njara Zafimehy, Elisa Sabbion, Laura Torres, Debbie Dreyfuss, Constantine Christodoulou, Kate Maleski, Pierre-Arnold Camphuis, Farah Jashanmal, Peggye Totozafy, Frederique Lonvis, Kawita Niwatananun, Mart Laohavoravudhikul, Alice Bouriez, Camille Voisin, Sara Kianpour, Shuchi Kothari, Cecile Hyafil Guillerme, Ben Golden, Lisa Morris, Anita Kirpalani, Carly Heinz, Olyvia Zarchin, Kate Riordan . . . an immense thank-you for all your hard work and your amazing development. Epic would be nothing without you.

To my former teams at Phonevalley and Scroon, it's thanks to you that I have the means to fulfill my ambitions. . . . Thanks also to Maurice Levy, Frédéric Joseph, David Kenny, Ariel Marciano, Stéphane Estryn, and Colin Kinsella at Publicis, and to Frank Boulben, Andrew Bocking, and David Proulx at Blackberry. And to my friend and lawyer Benjamin Kanovitch.

Lastly, to my blisce/ team, in particular my longtime right hand and partner Charles-Henri Prevost, Sam Giber, Othmane Sghir, Romain Sion, Milca Morat, Soline Kauffmann-Tourkestansky, and Himanish Shah, who made this crazy adventure possible with their expertise and hard work.

I would also like to thank all the clients and partners at my various companies who trusted me when I told them about a technological future that was difficult to imagine at the time.

To my whole family, thank you for surrounding us with so much love.

And to my second family, my friends: Morgann and Clémence Lesné, T.G. and Nicelle Herrington, Xavier and Cecile Herman, Jim Patrelle, Lionel and Géraldine Cottu, Edward and Carol Roussel, Bertrand and Mathilde Thomas, Christopher and France Descours, Jane Gering, Huy and Tram Ahn Nguyen Trieu, Marc and Pauline Levy, Alexandra and Aleksander Dembinski, Sameer and Francine Deen, Jim Hedges, Mathilde and Jean-Luc Moreau: I am so lucky to have you all around me.

To all the donors (individuals and companies), pledgers, and Epic ambassadors who have joined us with their desire to share and to improve the system. You give not only money but a great deal of hope—thank you all.

A very big thank-you to all the amazing Epic Ambassadors who are supporting us in our Epic journey: Bertrand Badré,

Christophe Bavière, Pierre Beaufils, Gonzalve Bich, John-Alexander Bogaerts, John Borthwick, Frank Boulben, Bruno Bouygues, Nathalie Boy de la Tour, Sumir Chadha, Emmanuel Chain, Gina and Christophe d'Ansembourg, Bracken Darrell, Vincent Dassault, Sameer Deen, Sebastien Deletaille, Philippe D'Ornano, Ian D'Souza, Boris Derichebourg, Fred Destin, Gad Elmaleh, Emmanuelle Errera, Tony Estanguet, Anne-Sophie Eymeoud, Loic Fery, Rowan Finnegan, Tom Franco, Ségolène Gallienne, Bernard Gault, Isabelle Giordano, Fabrice Grinda, Benoist Grossmann, James Hedges, Morgan Hermand-Waiche, TG Herrington, Sam Hodges, Chieh Huang, Todd Jacobson, Thierry Jadot, Philippe Journo, Edward Kim, Michael Kim, Laurent and Claire Koscielny, Morgann Lesné, Phil Libin, Zander Lurie, Jillian Manus, Kevin Mayer, Grand Corps Malade, Cédric Meeschaert, Doug Mellinger, Arieh Mimran, Nachson Mimran, Henri Moissinac, Jean Moueix, Gilles Mougenot, Huy and Tram Anh Nguyen Trieu, Jen O'Neal, Neil Parikh, Bruno Pavlovsky, Olivier Perier, Romain Peugeot, Bertrand Piccard, Dominique Piotet, Arnaud de Puyfontaine, Massimo Quattrocchi, Sonali de Rycker, Ian Rogers, Melinda Rogers, Alexandre de Rothschild, Angélique de Rougé, Edward Roussel, Frédéric Rozé, David Scott, Pierre-Antoine de Selancy, Emmanuel Seugé, Carol Solvay, Hope Taitz, Ronny Turiaf, Jacques Veyrat, Philip von Wulffen, Cole Zucker.

Thank you to our partner organizations, who help us in our Epic selection process.

To all those who give their time for free so that Epic can meet its ambitious objectives . . . thank you.

And, of course, my greatest admiration goes to the social entrepreneurs who dedicate their lives to improving our present.

Tenderest thanks to my children, Louis, Alice, Blanche, and Georges: you are my greatest joy.

And finally an immense thank-you to my wife Florence for her trust and her love.